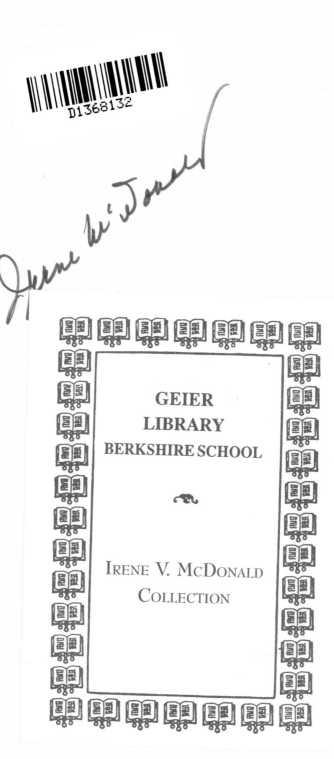

THE NERD

THE NERD

by

Larry Shue

Nelson Doubleday, Inc.
Garden City, N.Y.

For John Dillon.
No, wait a minute. No—
For James Pickering.

THE NERD was first presented by the Milwaukee Repertory Theater (John Dillon, Artistic Director) in April, 1981. It was directed by John Dillon; the set design was by Hugh Landwehr; costume design was by Colleen Muscha; the lighting design was by Dawn Chiang; the properties director was Sandy Struth; the production stage manager was Robert Goodman; and the stage manager was Robin Rumpf. The cast, in order of appearance, was as follows:

WILLUM CUBBERT	Larry Shue
TANSY McGINNIS	Kristine Thatcher
AXEL HAMMOND	Daniel Mooney
WARNOCK WALDGRAVE	Henry Strozier
CLELIA WALDGRAVE	Rose Pickering
THOR WALDGRAVE	Matthew Knuth
RICK STEADMAN	James Pickering

THE NERD was subsequently presented by the Royal Exchange Theatre Company in Manchester, England, in April, 1982. It was directed by Braham Murray; the production was designed by Johanna Bryant; the lighting was by Clive Odom; and the sound was by Tim Foster and George Glossop. The cast was as follows:

WILLUM	David Horovitch
AXEL	Gary Waldhorn
TANSY	Shelley Borkum
WALDGRAVE	Don Henderson
CLELIA	Sally Gibson
THOR	Matthew Barker/Oliver Findlay
RICK	Derek Griffiths

THE NERD was presented by Kevin Dowling & Joan Stein, Melvyn J. Estrin, Susan Rose, Gail Berman and Lynn Dowling in its New York premiere at the Helen Hayes Theatre on March 22, 1987. It was directed by Charles Nelson Reilly; the set design was by John Lee Beatty; costume design by Deborah Shaw; lighting design by Dennis Parichy; and the sound was by Timothy Helgeson. The production stage manager was Robert T. Bennett.

WILLUM	Mark Hamill
TANSY	Patricia Kalember
AXEL	Peter Riegert
WALDGRAVE	Wayne Tippit
CLELIA	Pamela Blair
THOR	Timmy Geissler
RICK	Robert Joy

THE NERD

Characters

Willum Cubbert
Tansy McGinnis
Axel Hammond
Warnock Waldgrave
Clelia Waldgrave
Thor Waldgrave
Rick Steadman

Place

Terre Haute, Indiana

Time

Act I
November 4, 1981

Act II
Scene 1: Six Days Later
Scene 2: The Following Day

ACT ONE

ACT I

As the lights come up, we find ourselves in a large, friendly room, early evening. A large window and doorway afford us a view of a wooden porch/balcony, and of autumn trees—oaks and maples—beyond. Treetops, actually, since we are on the second floor. The feeling is one of adventurous rusticity, rather as if we were in a treetop ourselves while still possessing all the comforts. Crusoe, Crichton, or the Family Robinson would, we feel, have approved. We notice hand-fashioned bookshelves, and framed watercolors of buildings—some of them commissioned architect's renderings, others more fanciful—all inspired by past styles, and all quite good. There is also a fireplace, a sofa, an easy-chair and a coffeetable. On an end-table, Stage Center, is the telephone and an answering machine—a particularly gifted one, with remote and intercom capabilities. The room, we shall see, does service as dining room, workroom, saloon and club for the house's three inhabitants, though strictly speaking it is the living room of only one—our protagonist, Willum. After a moment, we hear the clatter of feet on the wooden stair outside. They belong to Willum, and we know by their heavy crescendo that he is grateful to return to his sanctuary. Willum enters tiredly, briefcase in hand, and switches on the lights.

TANSEY & AXEL: *(Leaping from behind the furniture.)* SURPRISE!

WILLUM: *(Not displeased to see them.)* Oh, hi.

AXEL: "Oh, hi." Terrific. *(To* TANSEY.) Half an hour down there, I'll never be able to straighten this leg again, and for what? "Oh, hi."

TANSEY: *(To* WILLUM.) All right, we didn't surprise you at all, right?

WILLUM: *(Affably.)* Well, you know, when a fella gets to be my age—.

TANSEY: Oh, right—thirty-four, now. There's no fooling you.

WILLUM: That's right.

AXEL: Jaded old bastard.

TANSY: Sit yourself down, what am I thinking of? Sit, I'll get a blanket for your legs.

AXEL: *(Proffering his gift—a bottle in a plain brown bag.)* Here.

WILLUM: Now, I said no presents.

AXEL: *(Starting to take it back.)* Well, if you insist—.

WILLUM: Gimme it! *(Admiringly, as he gingerly removes the brown paper.)* Where'd you get this *wrapping* paper? *(Decisively.)* This gets saved. *(Sees bottle.)* Ohhhhh? Axel—a bottle of whiskey—practically full.

AXEL: It's com*plete*ly full! *(He can't help glancing at the bottle, however.)* You son of a bitch. "Practically full" . . .

WILLUM: *(Taking the bottle to the bar, he starts to sort through his mail.)* So why'd you come up so early? I gotta shower, and Waldgrave's coming over—.

AXEL: I've got an assignment tonight. Couldn't get out of it.

WILLUM: What's opening tonight?

AXEL: *(Consulting his notebook.)* At Theatre Now, the world premiere of *Drums Along the Wabash.*

WILLUM: Catchy title.

AXEL: *I'm* looking forward to it.

WILLUM: I'll watch for your review.

AXEL: You want to read it now?

TANSY: Here's your birthday card. *(She hands him an envelope and disappears into the kitchen, talking.)* We thought you'd be tired, we came up to get things started—you know, straighten up a little, make the salad—.

AXEL: Inflate all the whoopee cushions—.

WILLUM: All the niceties, right.

AXEL: That's right. *(Into the answering machine mike.)* Talking now to Will Cubbert, Terre Haute, Indiana's most promising young middle-aged architect; sir, how about telling our radio family your favorite sexual position?

WILLUM: *(Soberly, after a moment's contemplation.)* Third from the top, I guess.

AXEL: Uh-hunh.

TANSY: *(Entering with another large bowl.)* Did you read your card?

WILLUM: *(Referring to bowl.)* What's this?

TANSY: Three-bean salad.

WILLUM: Well, Tansy—?

TANSY: I thought we'd eat in here by the fire, and then if it gets crowded we can spill out onto the porch. *(She returns to the kitchen.)*

WILLUM: *(To AXEL.)* Did you do any of this?

AXEL: Me prepare food? Right, babe. You eat my food, you'll spill out onto the porch. Spill out onto the carpet.

WILLUM: *(Opening TANSY's envelope and reading the contents.)* "Happy Birthday, 8-year-old"! Pretty cruel, Tansy!

TANSY: *(Offstage.)* Keep reading!

WILLUM: *(Reading a second card from the same envelope.)* "Now that you are ten"! All right, I get it. "Hi, Mister Six-year-old!" *(He quickly looks through the others.)* "Two", "Five"—"Three". Okay.

TANSY: *(Entering with an enormous tray of macaroni salad, which she places on the coffee table.)* I couldn't find one that said "thirty-four", so I got six that added up.

WILLUM: *(Almost simultaneously.)* —that added up. Sure. *(Studying cards.)* God! I'm six little kids. *(He discovers a folded piece of stationery, and begins reading it to himself.)*

AXEL: *(Seeing salad.)* Christ, Tansy, you think you made enough macaroni salad?

TANSY: *(The tough cookie.)* Hey—button it, meathead.

AXEL: Now I know why there's a nationwide macaroni shortage. Terrible thing. I passed two little Brownie Scouts outside, crying their eyes out because they didn't have anything to make their necklaces out of.

WILLUM: *(Still looking at note.)* Aw, Tansy. *(Rereads it.)* Tansy, this really is nice.

TANSY: *(A little too busy and cheerful.)* Isn't that a nice little poem? I just came across that, and it made me think of you.

WILLUM: Oh, me. C'm'ere. *(They hug.)* Thank you, sweetie.

TANSY: *(Quietly.)* Perfectly all right.

WILLUM: *(Still hugging, he sighs.)* Oh. . . . Hell. *(Another moment, then he hastens to the bedroom, pulling off his tie.)*

AXEL: *(Brightly.)* Well! I guess you cheered *him* up!

TANSY: *(Watching after WILLUM, concerned.)* All right, I'm doing my best, okay?

AXEL: *(Referring to the note.)* So what have we here?

TANSY: Never mind.

AXEL: One more little endearment to make it that much tougher on him when you're gone?

TANSY: That wasn't my intention.

AXEL: Come on. You know you're not doing the guy any favors with that kind of stuff. I'm gonna hate watching a perfectly good landlord walking around with his guts scrambled because some little brown-eyed patootie decided to toss him an extra couple of macaroons before she hit the road.

TANSY: Axel—.

AXEL: The guy used to be a pretty good laugher, I don't know if you remember.

TANSY: It's his birthday.

AXEL: So give him a tie. *(Pause. She turns away.)* Or else give him what he really wants. (TANSY *shakes her head.)* The guy's thirty-four, for God's sake—he needs somebody to look after him in his dotage.

TANSY: Not me.

AXEL: Come on. Does Washington really need one more weather girl?

TANSY: Ax—I am leaving here one week from tomorrow, and nothing, but *noth*ing—.

AXEL: Hey. Hey.

TANSY: Look—oh, I know how I must look to you—like a parody of the New Woman, casting off her chains to go be the Washington Weather Girl—.

AXEL: I didn't say that. You put it awfully well, but I didn't say that—.

TANSY: And all right, so maybe it's not the loftiest goal ever pursued by womankind, or anything, but to me it happens to be that damn thing —that one chance that comes along in your life that you just gotta grab, 'cause if you don't, then before you know it, your eyes glaze over—and whatever or whoever you gave it up for, you start to resent. And I'm not gonna do that to Willum.

AXEL: Some favor you're doing him. "Willum—there's something bigger than us—a wonderful something called—meteorology."

TANSY: Willum will be all right.

AXEL: Think so?

TANSY: He's told me so.

AXEL: What does he know? Does he know you sneak up here every day and untangle this place?

TANSY: He's just been busy with his hotel—and he needed someone—.

AXEL: So, what, when you're gone he won't still need someone?

TANSY: Oh, I should give up my career to shelve a man's books?

AXEL: All right, so he's a little sloppy. I mean, if that's what you don't like about him—.

TANSY: There's nothing I don't like. Willum is wonderful; he's talented, he's the gentlest man I've ever known, he's—he could use a little gumption, I think, but—.

AXEL: "Gumption"? You've said that before. What is that? What is "gumption"?

TANSY: Just, something people have.

AXEL: I don't think so. Not anymore. I think they found the cure. It's like neuralgia. Who was the last person you ever heard of having "gumption"? Marjorie Main, right?

TANSY: All right.

AXEL: So now, what—Willum can't be perfect for you without "gumption"?

TANSY: No. Please—let him be imperfect. Somebody perfect right now would really louse things up. Willum has his hotel, I've got my

Weather Girl, so that's that. And besides, here I am, fresh out of one relationship, I've got no business—.

AXEL: Fresh? *Fresh?* It's two *years,* Tansy, that what you call *fresh?*

TANSY: Well—.

AXEL: I'll remember never to send you out for seafood.

TANSY: Fresh enough. Fresh in memory.

AXEL: Come on. So you once came close to marrying a bastard.

TANSY: Interesting bastard, I tell you that.

AXEL: Interesting to the vice squad, maybe.

TANSY: He was gifted. He could make people laugh.

AXEL: Too many appetites, that was his trouble. Cravings for things— *evil* things—booze, dope . . . people in show business. Candy-stripers. . . .

TANSY: Oh, I could've put up with all that, I think. That hunger. That wasn't really the problem.

AXEL: I never liked the man.

TANSY: That, I think, was the problem. (AXEL *laughs.*) If you didn't like him, there wasn't much hope for me, was there?

AXEL: *(Having lit a cigarette, he flings the match through the doorway toward the trees.)* Burn, you goddam trees! Burn!

TANSY: *(She puts both hands behind his neck.)* But I'll tell you something. He may not deserve it, and I know he doesn't want it, *(Quietly.)* but I'd like him to know he will be missed, too.

AXEL: *(The briefest moment, and then he greets a bottle on the bar as if it were an old comrade.)* Jack! *(To* TANSY.) Excuse me, will ya, honey? Jack! Jack Daniels! Where the hell you *been,* babe? *(He pours himself a generous shot. Still talking to the liquid.)* Have you had anything to eat? Well, try some of my *stomach* lining! *(He downs the glassful. Beatifically.)* He was a stranger, and I took him in.

TANSY: You're a hard man, Axel Hammond.

AXEL: Really? Am I good to find?

TANSY: You remember something I asked you the other night, at the Hallowe'en party?

AXEL: The Hallowe'en—was that *you?*

TANSY: I asked you—.

AXEL: You looked *just* like Petunia Pig.

TANSY: I asked if you'd ever done an anonymous favor, you remember that?

AXEL: Yes, I remember. It cut me to the quick, too.

TANSY: D'you remember what your answer was?

AXEL: Made me feel like the Marquis de Sade, or Scrooge—.

TANSY: You said—.

AXEL: Or Nixon, or somebody.

TANSY: You said, "An anonymous favor? Well—what would be in it for me?"

AXEL: Sure. So what?

TANSY: I guess all I'm saying is, creep—that I'd feel easier about leaving here if I could see you once just go crazy and *do* something for somebody.

AXEL: *(As Bill Sykes.)* Not this bloke. A villain I be, and a villain I'll stay.

TANSY: You're not either a villain. You're a little self-destructive. Possibly a little pretentious, but I don't think—.

AXEL: Pre*ten*tious?

TANSY: Well, yes.

AXEL: Pretentious? *Moi?*

TANSY: Where did I see that? *Reader's Digest,* right?

AXEL: My God. It's frightening. How could I have even thought of taking up with a woman who knew all my sources? It was just because you lived in the next apartment, I think; you were the only vice within walking-distance.

WILLUM: *(Reentering in fresh clothes.)* Did I check my messages? I didn't check my messages. *(He takes a remote control "beeper" from his hanging coat, "beeps" it once, and the answering-machine tape immediately begins replaying. He puts the beeper down on the table below the couch.* TANSY *goes into the kitchen.)*

WILLUM'S VOICE: *(On tape.)* Hello, hello. This is Willum Cubbert. November fourth. Hope you had a happy Hallowe'en. Uh, we're having a birthday sort of thing here tonight after supper, so drop by if you can—no presents, please. Uh, I'll be out most of the day—.

AXEL: You're not supposed to say that, you know.

WILLUM: What?

AXEL: That you're out. That's an open invitation to thieves.

WILLUM: Oh.

WILLUM'S VOICE. *(Continuing under.)* —but I should be back by six. If you beat me here, come on in; the door's always open. (AXEL *gives up.)* If you want to leave a message, wait'll you hear the tone, okay? *(Tone sounds.)*

WINK'S VOICE: Yeah, this is Wink. Hi, big fella. I got hung up at the
zoo with Pinky and the kids, and we may not make it, but—happy
birthday. See ya.

WILLUM: Okay. . . .

AXEL: *(Wincing.)* "Wink" and "Pinky"? *(Tone sounds. We hear a confused voice, perhaps* RICK*'s, say "uh-h-h . . . ," then a throat clear-
ing, then a phone hanging up. Tone sounds again.)*

RED'S VOICE: *(Aging, avuncular, Southwestern.)* Hey, son. This is Red
Graham again. Talk to me some more about this Alexandria thing,
will you? I can't see anybody else but you for that job, and I think
maybe we can improve the deal for you. Call me at the office, or leave
word with Doreen, all right? 'Preciate it. Happy birthday. Bye-bye.
(Tone sounds.)

WILLUM: *(Stopping machine.)* Call him back, I guess. *(He scribbles on a
pad.)* I surely hate phones.

AXEL: Job offer?

WILLUM: Yeah, this guy's been calling me for three days. He saw my
Colonial Village stuff and now wants me to do something just like it
for him. Housing development, big yawn.

AXEL: *(Smiling.)* Well, touch *you.*

WILLUM: Housing developments I can always get. But they're just—.

AXEL: They're not art?

WILLUM: Something like that. Anyway, the Regency job keeps me here
a year, and this Red Graham wants me in Alexandria next month,
so—.

AXEL: Alexan—? Alexandria, Vir*gin*ia? That's right across the river
from D.C., you know.

WILLUM: *(Looking up.)* Washington?

TANSY: *(Entering.)* What?

WILLUM: Uh, nothing. (WILLUM *hits the beeper, and the answering machine continues.)*

WALDGRAVE'S VOICE: Hi. I'll be out in your part of the country this afternoon with Thor and Clelia, picking apples. Clelia says it's supposed to strengthen our family bond.

AXEL: The family that picks together, sticks together.

WALDGRAVE'S VOICE: So I'll have them with me when I come by. If you've done those new exteriors, I'd like a look at those, too. *(Tone sounds.)*

AXEL: And a happy birthday to *you*, Mr. Waldgrave.

WILLUM: You know him?

AXEL: Not I. I have no truck with successful men. *(Tone sounds.)*

KEMP'S VOICE: *(Urbane, even affected, but with a hint of self-parody.)* Yes, this is Kemp Hall. I was told Axel Hammond could be reached here. If I don't hear from him by seven, tell him I'll proceed as directed. Thanks. And happy birthday, whoever you are.

WILLUM: Thank you. *(Tone sounds and* WILLUM *stops the machine.)* Who was that?

AXEL: One of the carny-folk.

TANSY: *(To* AXEL.*)* Your new friend?

AXEL: *(Nods.)* Kemp Hall. *(To* WILLUM.*)* Ever heard of him?

WILLUM: Don't think so.

AXEL: Damnedest character man you ever saw.

WILLUM: "Proceed as directed"—what was all that?

AXEL: You *don't* want to know.

WILLUM: *(Holding up a hand.)* Fine. *(Restarts the machine.)*

DEAN'S VOICE. Hi, Willy-Worm. Dean the Bean here.

AXEL: Dipstick.

DEAN'S VOICE. Four things. I just found your checkbook under my desk; I don't know when you lost it. *(After "under my desk", WIL-LUM checks his coat, discovering with mild surprise that his checkbook is, in fact, missing.)* Two, I can't come over tonight, but I'll get your checkbook to you tomorrow. Three, I *did* have a happy Hallowe'en, thanks muchly, and four—happy birthday. Goom-bye.

TANSY: Great! Small, intimate gathering—we can build a macaroni fort. *(Tone sounds.)*

RICK'S VOICE: *(Adenoidal, uncertain.)* William Cubbert? Uh, hi, this is Rick Steadman on the phone.

WILLUM: *(Mental block.)* Steadman. Rick Steadman—?

RICK'S VOICE: You said if I was ever over by you I should come over for a visit, and so . . . here I am, so I'll be comeen' over.

WILLUM: Rick *Stead*man! This is Rick Steadman!

TANSY: Who's Rick—. (WILLUM *shushes her.)*

RICK'S VOICE: When you said, "Happy Hallowe'en", was this a Hallowe'en party tonight, or what? I mean, are we supposed to dress up all nutty, and all? Let me know. *(Answering machine cuts off.)*

WILLUM: Wait! Where *are* you?

AXEL: Hallowe'en party? A few days late.

WILLUM: He didn't leave a number! Tansy!

TANSY: What?

WILLUM: Rick *Stead*man's coming!

TANSY: Who's Rick Steadman?

WILLUM: From Nam! *(To* AXEL.) Remember? The guy from Nam!

AXEL: Your good Samaritan?

WILLUM: I finally get to meet him!

TANSY: Someone you haven't seen since the army?

WILLUM: I've never seen him *ever.* This is the guy—I've told you how I got my purple heart, didn't I?

TANSY: I remember your saying you were wounded in the line of duty.

WILLUM: Well, sort of.

AXEL: You were a draftsman, right?

WILLUM: Right—safest job in the army. I was a draftsman for the Quartermaster Corps. I got sent to Nam to spend a year drawing pictures of officers' clubs. Fine. So I'm off the plane *maybe* forty-eight hours, by which time, never mind how, I've gotten myself into the middle of some rice field, VC country. I'm in dress uniform in a rainstorm, my collapsible PX umbrella has collapsed, I'm trying to find the road on a map that's turning into Malt-o-Meal in my hands —I'm totally lost. I'm so tired and disgusted I forget to be scared. And I start thinking of all these stupid war-movie quotes, and without realizing it I start saying them out loud. And I remember saying —"Well—it's a damn dirty job, but somebody's got to do it." Then I hear this sound, this loud, fluttering sound, like a playing card on a bicycle wheel? It's an AK-47. Next thing I know I'm sitting in a puddle, and even though I can't see myself through the mud, I realize intuitively I've been shot because there's all this great pain? And all I can think of is, I gotta let 'em know I'm a draftsman, right?—some-how, so they won't kill me. I'm trying to think of a universal sign for "draftsman", and that's when I pass out. I wake up, I'm in Japan, Navy hospital. Both my legs are in a cast; they look like two enor-mous cannoli, y'know? But I'm gonna be okay. Purple heart, honorable discharge. I'm going home. So what had happened—this guy, Rick Steadman, he was just a poor grunt, wounded himself, wounded in the arm, running from an attack that had backfired; but he saw me, and with his one good arm he dragged me a mile and a half through the jungle to his base camp—refused medical attention till I'd gotten everything I needed.

TANSY: Yep. That's brave.

WILLUM: And so, here I am, legs and all, thanks to him.

TANSY: And you never met?

WILLUM: No, we were both shipped right back. But I got his address from records and wrote him, and he wrote back, nice letter, he works in a factory, I think, in—someplace in Wisconsin, town with an Indian name, I can't remember—.

AXEL: Silverheels.

WILLUM: What?

AXEL: Nothing.

WILLUM: Anyway—*(Getting the joke.)* Silverheels, right. Silverheels, Wisconsin. Anyway—so I told him—"As long as I'm *alive,* you will have someone on this earth who will do *any*thing for you. I mean it. Money? A place to stay? *Any*thing.

TANSY: Of course.

WILLUM: Lately we're a little out-of-touch—it's just been Christmas cards and stuff, but . . . Gee. Rick Steadman.

AXEL: If this is a scam to wheedle me out of my last bottle of Dom Perignon, you've just done it. Be right back. *(Exits down stairs.)*

TANSY: *(To* WILLUM.*)* Pretty excited, huh, kid?

WILLUM: Well, *yeah.* And boy, I'm glad you're—I mean, I'm glad you could be here for this.

TANSY: Yeah. Me too. *(They are reaching out and squeezing hands now.* TANSY *grows especially pretty in supportive moments like this, and* WILLUM, *his goose cooked, moves toward her.)*

WILLUM: Tansy, Tansy—*(She ducks her head, albeit with some reluctance, and he must settle for gently bumping foreheads with her once or twice.)*

TANSY: I know. I know.

WILLUM: Okay. Okay.

AXEL: *(Returning with a bottle.)* I've been saving this for—*(Seeing their downcast looks, sepulchrally.)* "But lo! The Angel of Death had come among them." What happened? I was gone thirty seconds. *(We hear a car and see its lights play across the darkening window.)*

WILLUM: *(Snapping to.)* Rick—what if that's Rick? What should we do?

AXEL: Let's make sure he'll remember you. Sit on the floor, and I'll cover your legs with shrimp sauce.

WILLUM: Very funny. I *mean* it.

TANSY: *(Looking out.)* It's Mr. Waldgrave.

WILLUM: What? Oh—*(On porch.)* Hi! Come up! Come up! (WILLUM *holds the door open for* WALDGRAVE, *who carries a mesh bag full of small, green apples. The last time Mr.* WALDGRAVE *smiled was forty-seven years ago, and then it was gas.)*

WALDGRAVE: Here. These are for you.

WILLUM: Oh, thanks.

WALDGRAVE: You ought to be able to eat 'em in a few days. *(To* TANSY.) How are you? Tammy?

TANSY: Tansy.

WALDGRAVE: Right.

WILLUM: Tansy McGinnis you've met. Axel, this is the man who's letting me design his hotel—.

AXEL: I've seen you on the finance page. The self-made man. Warnock Waldgrave, rags-to-riches—.

WALDGRAVE: *(Holding up a hand.)* Ticky.

AXEL: Pardon?

WALDGRAVE: Ticky. Call me Ticky.

AXEL: Well, I'd rather swallow glass, but if you insist—.

WILLUM: Axel Hammond, friend and tenant. *(He smiles and exits to porch.)*

WALDGRAVE: *(Offering hand.)* Axel?

AXEL: *(Shaking hands.)* Gumbo. Just call me Gumbo.

TANSY: Don't you dare. (WALDGRAVE *chuckles uncertainly.* WILLUM *opens the door again and in comes* CLELIA WALDGRAVE *with their eight-year-old son,* THOR. CLELIA *is a picture of tasteful, studied patience, but not because her life is devoid of anxiety. As for* THOR, *we know that there are good little boys; there are also precocious little boys, which is to say bad little boys whom we can somehow find it in our hearts to forgive.* THOR *is neither.* THOR *is a monster, and might well usurp the action from our other characters were he not soon relegated to another room.)*

WALDGRAVE: Dear, this is Willum, Tandy, and—.

TANSY: Tansy.

WALDGRAVE: Tansy, and—Gumbo?

TANSY: Axel.

WALDGRAVE: Axel, right. (AXEL *shrugs at a wondering* WILLUM.) Uh, my wife Clelia—.

WILLUM: *(To* CLELIA, *warmly.)* Oh, yes. *(Trying to remember.)* Now, what is it you're involved in?

CLELIA: *(Very slowly and clearly.)* I work with slow learners.

WILLUM: Oh. Uh, right. You know Tansy?

CLELIA: *(Nods.)* Tansy?

TANSY: Hi.

WALDGRAVE: And my son Thor.

WILLUM: Thor?

THOR: *(Whining.)* Daa-yad!

WALDGRAVE: What, son?

THOR: *(Whining.)* I hate it here.

WALDGRAVE: No you don't, son.

THOR: Daaa-yad! I do *toooo!* (He begins to whimper. AXEL *has quietly removed a poker from the fireplace.)*

TANSY: Axel! *(He replaces the poker.)*

THOR: You promised me I could go play with A.J. Morovek!

WILLUM: Who?

THOR: Pleeeeee-ease?

CLELIA: A.J. Morovek. His little friend.

AXEL: He has a little friend named A.J. Morovek? Funny—all *Willum's* friends have names like Pinky and Winky and Dean the Bean.

(To WALDGRAVE.*)* Doesn't that strike you as funny, Mr.—uh, Ticky? (THOR *starts sobbing loudly now, collapsing under the weight of his grief till he is being upheld only by* WALDGRAVE*'s grip on his arm.)*

WALDGRAVE: *(To* CLELIA.*)* What's gotten into him all of a sudden?

CLELIA: I can't conceive.

AXEL: We all wish.

WALDGRAVE: I don't understand it. He's never done anything like this before. (THOR *stamps on* WALDGRAVE*'s foot, runs screaming into the bedroom, and slams the door.* WALDGRAVE *grabs the doorknob, but the door is locked.) Damn* it, Clelia, he's done it again! Thor! Thor, come out of there!

CLELIA: Ticky—*reason* with him.

WILLUM: Is there anything I can do?

AXEL: You get the mortar, I'll get the bricks.

WALDGRAVE: Thor! Come out or I'm going to break your arms.

CLELIA: Ticky! Please—if you treat him as an adult, he'll respond as an adult.

WALDGRAVE: *(Running a hand through his hair.)* Yeah, okay. Thor? Thor, come out of there and I'll give you thirty bucks.

CLELIA: Ticky!

WALDGRAVE: *(To* CLELIA.*)* It's okay, I can spare it. *(To* THOR.*)* Thirty bucks, son. That's five more than last time.

CLELIA: Ticky! You've offered him *money,* to—?

WALDGRAVE: Honey, let me handle this, dammit! *(Angrily explaining.)* I'm here, a., for *business,* and b., for *fun!* I'm in no mood for psychology! *(To* THOR.*)* How about it, son? Thirty bucks. Straight business deal.

THOR: *(Offstage.)* Fifty.

WALDGRAVE: What?

THOR: *(Offstage.)* Fifty dollars and I come out!

WALDGRAVE: You little bloodsucker! I'll see you in hell first!

WILLUM: Uh, can I take your coats or anything?

WALDGRAVE: *(To* THOR.*)* Okay, buddy! I can stonewall as well as you can! I'm going to enjoy myself out here with these real nice people and this great-looking macaroni salad. I just hope there's stuff in there that's that much fun!

THOR: *(Offstage.) There* is. (WILLUM *gives* AXEL *a worried look.)*

WILLUM: Oh, I'm sure everything will be fine. Here, want to see the new kitchen?

WALDGRAVE: Okay. *(To* THOR.*)* I'll deal with you later, pal! You're a big, fat disappointment to me, I hope you know that!

CLELIA: Come on, Ticky.

WALDGRAVE: *(Exiting with* WILLUM, TANSY *and* CLELIA *toward the kitchen.)* Damn kid. Damn kid'll be president of General Motors someday, mark my words. *(And they are out.* AXEL *watches them leave, then crosses to phone, whistling "Happy Birthday to You." The receiver rests on the answering machine. He dials, we hear it ring and another machine answer.)*

KEMP'S VOICE: This is Kemp Hall. I'm tied up at the moment, but if you'd care to leave your—. (AXEL *pushes a button on the beeper, and* KEMP's *voice stops. We hear a dial tone in its place.)*

AXEL: Okay, sugar. *(Looking for the right button.)* So how do I hang up? *(He picks a button, pushes it, and we hear the tape on* WILLUM's

*machine rewinding. He pushes another button, muttering "Hell." The
machine starts replaying midway through the tape, slowing down as it
does.)*

WILLUM'S VOICE: Hello, hello. This is Willum—.

AXEL: *(Pushing yet another button.)* Hell, hell. *(The tape speeds forward. He tries another button.)*

WILLUM'S VOICE: *(Getting slower.)* —t'll—you—hear—the—tone.
Okay?

WILLUM: *(Having entered during this.)* What's the news in here?

AXEL: Robbie the Robot's going into self-destruct, here. (WILLUM
moves to the beeper.)

WINK'S VOICE: *(Very slow.)* Yeah . . . this . . . is . . . Wink . . .

WILLUM: *(Pushing the magic button which stops the tape and shuts off
the machine.)* Yeah, it does that. Take it back in, I guess. Any word
from—? *(He jerks his thumb toward the bedroom.)*

AXEL: From little Damien? No, he's been pretty quiet.

WILLUM: *(Grabbing some renderings.)* I just hope his daddy likes my
pictures.

AXEL: These the new ones?

WILLUM: Yep.

AXEL: *(Looking them over.)* Less is more, huh?

WILLUM: That's what the man says. What do you think?

AXEL: I hate to be an "I-liked-it-better-before", but—.

AXEL & WILLIAM: "—I liked it better before."

WILLUM: Okay. Well, I've kept a few things.

AXEL: Yeah.

WILLUM: You staying in here?

AXEL: Me and Jack, yeah.

WILLUM: Yell if Rick comes, will you? (WILLUM *exits.*)

AXEL: Sure. *(We hear* THOR *again, as* TANSY *and* CLELIA *enter.)*

THOR: *(Offstage.)* BEEE—BO! BEEE-BO! BEEE-BO!

AXEL: *(Grabbing the Jack Daniels bottle and escaping to the kitchen.)* Poster child for Planned Parenthood. *(And he is gone.)*

CLELIA: *(Seeing the bedroom door is still locked.)* Oh, dear. Still hiding.

TANSY: Oh, he'll be out soon.

CLELIA: I suppose. It's just that Thor becomes so difficult sometimes— and then Ticky gets angry, and then angry with *me,* then it's all I can do to—. *(She begins picking through her purse.)*

TANSY: I know, I know.

CLELIA: *(On the verge of tears.)*—and then Thor gets that much more stubborn and whiney; sometimes it's more than I can—deal with. These men—.

TANSY: Ain't it the truth.

CLELIA: Well—you're a blessing, anyway. *(Unable to find what she's been searching her purse for.)* Oh, dear. I wonder if I could ask you— I wonder if you have anything—?

TANSY: A hanky?

CLELIA: No—I wonder if you have anything I could—break.

TANSY: *(After a moment.)* What? Break?

CLELIA: *(Apologetically.)* Yes, just—something small. Sometimes it's all that will help. It sounds silly, I suppose—.

TANSY: Oh, no, no. Uh, let's see—*(Looking around.)* well—anything in particular?

CLELIA: No . . . A little saucer, something.

TANSY: A little saucer. Uh—fine.

CLELIA: Nothing expensive, now. I can do without.

TANSY: Don't be silly. I don't want you to sit here all night with—without anything to break.

CLELIA: I usually carry little Woolworth's saucers, but I seem to have used my last one at the orchard.

TANSY: *(Finding a demitasse saucer.)* Here, will this do? It's just a demitasse.

CLELIA: No, that's fine. *(A little sadly.)* Those are my favorites. *(She takes a handkerchief and a small butter knife from her purse, spreads the handkerchief neatly on the table, lays the saucer on it face down and, using several small, efficient strokes, pulverizes the dish with the knife handle. She sighs.)*

TANSY: Another?

CLELIA: No, I'll pass. Thanks.

THOR: *(Offstage.)* Gambee, gambee, ga-a-a-a-a-a-a-a-a-a-a-amby MOE! *(There is a crash.)*

CLELIA: Maybe later.

TANSY: I may join you. (AXEL *enters from the kitchen.*)

AXEL: *(Politely, to* TANSY.*)* I just want to make sure—is the cider supposed to be boiling all over everything and turning black and hard?

TANSY: The cider! Oh, God! *(The three of them exit into the kitchen. After a moment, the bedroom door opens slightly as* THOR *checks out the living room. The coast being clear, out he comes, festooned with* WILLUM's *flowered boxer shorts, bathrobe, soap-on-a-rope, and so on. He brandishes a flashlight as if it were some sort of a laser weapon.)*

THOR: Bee-bee-bee-bee-bee—! Bimgimo the Great! *(In a gruff sing-song, stamping around majestically like a Japanese movie monster.)* I step on the enemies! *(There is a knock at the door.* THOR *hides behind the sofa, but when the knock recurs decides to answer it. Opening the door.)* Who calls at the house of the great—? *(Before us in the doorway, a small piece of paper in hand, stands* RICK STEADMAN. *He is dressed in a Hallowe'en costume which is really needlessly horrible, never mind the fact that it is several days too late—the Creature from the Black Lagoon, perhaps, after a tussle with the propeller of an ore-boat—glistening wounds on a scaly, green body, one eye semi-detached, and so on. The outfit must have cost him ninety dollars.)*

RICK: *(To* THOR, *who is momentarily transfixed by terror.)* Am I too late? I didn't know if this was—.

THOR: EEEEEEEEEEEEEEEEEEEE! *(He throws himself into the closet, slamming the door.)*

RICK: *(Lowering his voice, excitedly.)* Oh, okay. *(Crouching and looking quickly around.)* Where are we supposed to hide? Does it matter? *(No answer. Of course.)* Okay. *(He hides behind one of the large* U. *chairs. Several seconds pass. In the same loud whisper.)* When's he supposed to get here? *(Long pause.)* Anybody know? *(Pause.)* Okay. *(*WILLUM *and* WALDGRAVE *enter, studying a watercolor.)*

WALDGRAVE: So what are we talking? We're talking about four, five things, tops. That archway there, all that junk around the windows. Get rid of that, we're in business. What's your problem?

WILLUM: *(With difficulty.)* Yeah—I know, I just can't help feeling if we lose all that molding, see, it won't be—I mean, I'm afraid it's gonna start looking like a lot of other buildings, and—. *(*THOR *explodes out of the closet, clutching* WALDGRAVE *around the waist and hiding his face in* WALDGRAVE's *stomach.)*

WALDGRAVE: Son—! What is it? What's wrong? (THOR *just shakes his head.*) You're tickling me, son. Come on. Tell Daddy what's bothering you. (THOR *whispers squeakily in his ear, pointing at the door.*) A what? (THOR *whispers again.* WALDGRAVE *sits him down on the sofa. His tone is patient, fatherly.*) Now, son, you know. You know I put up with a lot, but—*(Turning* THOR *over his knee and spanking the daylights out of him.)* I—will—not—put—up—with—a—*liar!* (THOR *wails and runs back into the bedroom, slamming the door again.* CLELIA *has entered during the spanking.*)

CLELIA: Ticky—!

WALDGRAVE: *(Silencing her with a warning finger.)* Clelia—?

TANSY: *(Entering merrily with mugs of mulled cider.)* Well—are you two ready to show us a hotel?

WILLUM: *(Shushing her.)* Tansy—(AXEL *enters.*)

TANSY: What's happened?

WALDGRAVE: Nothing. My son has been watching too many Saturday morning cartoons, that's all.

AXEL: So that's why the only thing on him that moves is his mouth—I was wondering.

WALDGRAVE: Everything's under control now, so let's just—enjoy ourselves and have a good time. *(He seizes a cup of cider, clenching it like a grenade.)*

WILLUM: *(Hopefully.)* Well, sure. *(They all take cider and sit uneasily.)*

TANSY: *(After a pause.)* Well. *(Pause.)*

WILLUM: So. *(Another uncomfortable silence. Finally* RICK, *still in full costume, stands up behind the chair, studying his note.)*

RICK: *(Confused, even a little put out.)* Excuse me, is this twenty-two fifty-five River Road? *(Everyone reacts with alarm; there are involun-*

tary shouts. Cider is spilled. Everyone stares at RICK *for many moments, trying to recover from shock and to think what to say.)*

WILLUM: *(Finally.)* Uh—what? What?

RICK: *(Who never says his final g's.)* What's goeen' on?

WILLUM: What?

RICK: Why was I hideen'?

WILLUM: I—I—what do you mean?

WALDGRAVE: *(Taking over.)* What's going on?

RICK: That's what I want to know.

TANSY: Wait a minute—.

WALDGRAVE: Is this some kind of joke?

RICK: Do I look like I would be jokeen'? Who are you?

WILLUM: *(Realizing who he is.)* Rick Steadman!

RICK: You're Rick Steadman?

WILLUM: No, no! *You—you* are!

RICK: That's what I *thought. (He gives an ironic snort.)* I was gonna *say.*

WILLUM: *(To the others.)* It's Rick Steadman! Rick! It's me, it's Willum Cubbert!

RICK: Oh.

WILLUM: *(To the others.)* This man—this is the man that saved my life in Nam! *(Everyone relaxes on hearing this, and there are ad-libbed greetings: "Well, then!", "Hi, Rick!", "Hey, good goin'!", "Why'd you wanna save* him*? Heh, heh!"—and the like.)*

RICK: 'Cause I didn't think there would be more than one Rick Steadman, especially out here in the woods.

WILLUM: No, no, that was just—.

RICK: It's not that common of a name, y'know? Steadman, yes, okay. Granted. But not Rick Steadman.

WILLUM: Oh. *(Chuckles.)* Uh, listen, why don't you—?

RICK: I don't think I've ever even *heard* of another Rick *Stead*man.

WILLUM: No? Well, no, I guess me neither.

RICK: Oh, so that was just a joke then, right?

WILLUM: What?

RICK: Wait a minute. Why was I hideen'?

WILLUM: Uh—I don't know, Rick.

RICK: Okay. *(Shrugging goodnaturedly.)* If you don't know, I guess I don't know. *(Snorts.)* It's your house.

WILLUM: *(Gamely.)* Right, right. Uh, listen, why don't you take off your, uh, mask, and get comfortable?

RICK: Thanks.

AXEL: It's not midnight yet, but what the hell.

RICK: *(Pulling off the rubber head and placing it, face front, atop the answering machine.)* It's hot in there, believe me.

WILLUM: I'll bet.

RICK: *Real* hot.

WILLUM: Yeah, I'll bet.

RICK: *Mid*night?

WILLUM: Excuse me?

RICK: What?

WILLUM: Excuse me?

RICK: Sure. *(They stare at each other.)*

TANSY: *(To the rescue.)* Rick? Hi, Tansy McGinnis. (RICK *is still look-ing at* WILLUM.) This is Axel Hammond, and Warnock Waldgrave—

WALDGRAVE: *(Shaking* RICK's *hand.)* Ticky.

RICK: What?

TANSY: Right, I'm sorry. Ticky, this is Rick. Rick, Ticky.

WALDGRAVE: Pleasure.

RICK: *(Examining* WALDGRAVE's *"costume.")* What are you supposed to be?

WALDGRAVE: Well—I'm a businessman.

RICK: Oh. *(Mildly approving.)* Yeah, that's good.

TANSY: And Clelia Waldgrave—*(With some reluctance,* CLELIA *takes the scaly hand.)*

RICK: So what are you?

CLELIA: I—I'm a teacher.

RICK: *(Delighted.) Ha,* ha! A teacher, right! With your hair all pulled back and all, and stoopeen' all down, that's great! (CLELIA, *who hadn't realized she was "stooping all down," is a little wounded.)* Soo. I guess I'm the only monster. *(Again, everyone is tongue-tied.)* First they tried to sell me a pig. But I said I wasn't getteen' into no pig, even if it was the Queen of England.

WILLUM: Uh—.

RICK: So who was that answereen' the door? He was great!

WILLUM: Who?

RICK: You know, the little guy in the boxer shorts? Boxer shorts with flowers printed all over 'em?

CLELIA: Thor—it must have been Thor.

WALDGRAVE: Where would Thor get flowered boxer shorts?

TANSY: *(Laughing.)* Oh, those are Willum's—Willum has a pair like that. (WILLUM *looks at her.*) Probably.

RICK: So—is there a judgeen', or anything?

WILLUM: What? A judging?

RICK: For the costumes?

WILLUM: Uh, Rick—I mean, it's all right, but this wasn't really supposed to be a costume party.

RICK: *(To* WALDGRAVE *and* CLELIA, *snorting and rolling his eyes in goodnatured mock-exasperation.)* Oh, *great! Now* he tells us, right? Here Tocky goes out and buys this funny business costume, *(To* CLELIA.) and you spend all day, prob'ly, getteen' all dressed up like a little old teacher, and then what happens? We get here and he says "no costumes." Great!

WILLUM: It's not important—.

RICK: *(Still ribbing.)* Oh, sure, "It's not important," that's easy for *you* to say. You're not standeen' around all dressed up like a bunch of goofballs the way we are. Right, Tocky?

WALDGRAVE: Ticky!

RICK: What?

WALDGRAVE: Ticky! My name is Ticky!

RICK: Ticky. Oh. Okay. Right?

WALDGRAVE: Right *what?*

RICK: Right, Ticky?

WALDGRAVE: No, I'm saying what's the *question?*

RICK: What question?

WALDGRAVE: *(Pause. Almost at a loss.) What* question?

RICK: Right.

WALDGRAVE: Right *what?*

RICK: Tocky?

WALDGRAVE: *Ticky!*

RICK: Oh. *(Referring to costume.)* Could I get out of this, do you think?

WILLUM: What? Sure.

RICK: Oh, good. *(To the* WALDGRAVES, *as he removes his monster suit.)* I mean, I hate to stick you guys by yourselves, but I'm weareen' normal stuff under here, so I'm takeen' this off.

AXEL: And in the spring, when the cicada emerges from its cocoon . . . (RICK *has removed the suit, and now stands before us as we shall see him throughout the remainder of the evening—white shirt, tie, parted hair, and a pair of glasses which he sometimes repositions by wrinkling his nose. He does not wear the white socks we somehow expect, though the socks he does wear seem to be of different lengths and—yes—colors. Overall, the effect is one of near-adequacy. He holds out the costume.)*

RICK: Thanks. Who should I give this to?

TANSY: Here. *(She takes it.)* In the closet all right?

AXEL: You wouldn't want it to wrinkle.

RICK: Right. Thanks. (TANSY *has opened the closet and hangs the costume on the back side of the door.)* That's better.

WILLUM: Oh, you want to clean up or anything?

RICK: Sure, okay.

WILLUM: *(Leading him out through the kitchen area.)* Here. I'm sorry. *(They are gone.)*

AXEL: *You're* sorry.

TANSY: *(Ever the cheerful hostess.)* Well! That was certainly . . . unexpected.

CLELIA: Yes. . . .

WALDGRAVE: That guy saved somebody's life?

TANSY: He really did. Saved Willum's life.

AXEL: He must've been trying to kill him.

TANSY: No, now, he just—we just all got off to a kind of a bad start, that's all. He's probably—fine.

WALDGRAVE: Fine? He thought my wife and I were in Hallowe'en costumes. You call that fine?

TANSY: No, he was a little confused, that's all. Here, now, food's ready, everybody follow me! *(They are gone. After a moment or two, the bedroom door slowly opens, and out on all fours crawls THOR, looking nervously about. Presently he finds himself behind the coffee table, where his caution gives way to curiosity; he has discovered the "beeper." He picks it up, pushes a button, and the answering machine, now with the monster head upon it, starts playing where it stopped, still slow and ominous.)*

WINK'S VOICE: Hi . . . big . . . fella. . . ! I . . . got . . . hung . . . up . . . at . . . the . . . zooo. . . ! *(During this,* THOR *has slowly turned, almost against his will, to locate the origin of the voice. Seeing the monster head, he is seized with paralysis for a long moment after the spectre has finished its dark greeting, then shrieks again and flees once more to his bedroom sanctuary.* WILLUM *and* WALDGRAVE *enter, chatting, and the others, sans* RICK, *soon drift in behind. Everyone has a plate bearing an appetizing-looking Cornish hen, and things have generally settled down.)*

WILLUM: —the next thing I know I'm in a Naval hospital in Japan—honorable discharge, and I'm going home.

CLELIA: And you never met him?

WILLUM: Not till tonight.

CLELIA: My goodness.

WALDGRAVE: What line of business you in, Axel?

AXEL: Marketing. Yep. The old marketing game. Consumer market research, we call it.

TANSY: Axel—

AXEL: See, I advise manufacturers which one of their products they should eliminate as a result of poor consumer response. You see.

WALDGRAVE: *(Who still doesn't know how to take* AXEL. *And never will.)* Oh? Such as what?

AXEL: *(Expansively.)* Well, take 32 Flavors Ice Cream, for instance—well, 31 Flavors now—they were losing profits like crazy, couldn't figure it; I talked 'em into getting rid of their least popular flavor, and bingo.

WALDGRAVE: What was the flavor?

AXEL: Barium. Barium Crunch, I think they called it. It was pretty bad. It was sort of gray. Stank quite a bit.

TANSY: What are you, trying to make us all sick?

AXEL: Oh, then there was Doc Johnson's Marital Aids. They were—

TANSY: Drama critic! Axel's a drama critic for the paper, really.

WALDGRAVE: A drama critic? Then what was all that about marketing—?

TANSY: *(Gaily.)* Lies! All lies. Axel's little tragic flaw.

WALDGRAVE: Hm.

TANSY: Oh, you knew he was kidding.

WALDGRAVE: I had a pretty good idea. *(Like fun.)*

TANSY: I thought so.

WALDGRAVE: *(To* AXEL.) So you what? You get to see all the shows free?

AXEL: Just the "important" ones.

WALDGRAVE: Uh-huh. Ever see anything good?

AXEL: Nope.

TANSY: Axel tends to be a little embittered. See, he writes for the morning paper, so with his deadline he always has to miss the last half-hour of whatever he's reviewing. I mean, for all Axel knows, Hamlet gets the girl. Godot shows up. *He* doesn't know.

WALDGRAVE: What's—isn't there some gal in town doing some Shakespeare show with—I mean, without any—?

AXEL: Clothes on, yes, that's right—Andrea St. What's-her-name, down at the Grand. Two hours of classic monologues, unencumbered by clothing. I think it's called "Shakespeare in the Raw."

TANSY: *(Defensively.)* It's called "Shakespeare's Women;" it happens to be very effective, and very moving.

WALDGRAVE: *(To* AXEL.*)* How was that? Did you see her?

AXEL: Yeah. I covered her opening, which was more than she—no, I'm not gonna say it, I'm not gonna say it. (RICK *enters, having completed his ablutions, looking pretty much the same, except that he now trails a short length of toilet paper from one shoe.)*

WILLUM: There he is. (RICK *smiles wanly, strolls about. One by one the others notice the toilet paper, then politely decide to ignore it.)*

WALDGRAVE: Well—show business. We have a daughter, you've met her, Willum—

WILLUM: *(She's lovely.)* Gillian.

WALDGRAVE: —Gillian, and she's just seventeen yet, but she can play this—*(To* CLELIA.*)* What's it called—?

CLELIA: The piano?

WALDGRAVE: No, that music—that piece she plays.

CLELIA: Tchaikovsky's First Piano Concerto.

WALDGRAVE: Right, get this—she plays that on the piano, and accompanies herself on the harp.

TANSY: Really?

CLELIA: Oh, you should see her.

WALDGRAVE: *(Demonstrating vaguely.)* She puts the harp right here, reaches past it, and plays both things at once. *(Chuckles proudly.)* Don't ask me how. It's the damnedest thing. *(Everyone makes amazed, admiring sounds.)*

RICK: *(Idly.)* Yeah . . . They all go through that. (WALDGRAVE *glares.)*

TANSY: *(Saving things again.)* Oh, here's a plate for you, Rick.

RICK: *(Taking it.)* Thanks. What is this?

TANSY: Rock Cornish hen.

RICK: Right, right. That's what I thought. 'Cause guess what?

TANSY: What?

RICK: This is what I had for lunch.

TANSY: Oh. . . .

RICK: *(Regretfully.)* Yep.

TANSY: Well—just, you know, have whatever you like. I mean, don't feel bad about leaving it.

RICK: Okay. *(Picking up the hen and looking about.)* Is there a trash can somewhere?

TANSY: *(Rescuing RICK's hen.)* Here, let me take it. Somebody'll want it later, I'm sure.

RICK: Okay.

TANSY: *(Heading for the kitchen.)* Pop it in the warmer. Could I— would you like something else instead? A hot dog would be easy, or I could even make spaghetti.

RICK: 'Kay.

TANSY: Which?

RICK: Spaghetti?

TANSY: *(A little dazed.)* I'll be back in—ten or fifteen minutes. *(She exits.)*

WILLUM: *(Shouts.)* Need any help?

TANSY: *(Offstage. Cheerfully.)* No!

WALDGRAVE: *(Starting to eat.)* Well, this is really something.

CLELIA: Yes, isn't it lovely?

TANSY: *(Reenters with a plate of devilled eggs.)* It's a good thing I had to go back in; I forgot to put out the devilled eggs.

WALDGRAVE: They look great, too.

CLELIA: Oh, yes.

WILLUM: Mmm, sure do.

WALDGRAVE: Suddenly I'm *hungry.*

TANSY: *(Beams quickly, then goes back to the kitchen.)* Good old Mom's recipe. Back in a minute. *(Everyone has a devilled egg. An appreciative bite or two is taken.)*

RICK: *(Studying his egg. Philosophically.)* It's hard to believe, you know? *(The others look at him.)* Just a little while ago, these were all inside some birds. *(Everybody succinctly finds a place to deposit his or her egg for the remainder of the evening.* AXEL *tosses his gracefully into the fireplace.* RICK *thoughtfully eats his, but no one is really able to watch.)*

WALDGRAVE: *(To* WILLUM.) You were saying something?

WILLUM: I don't remember. *(Pause. Some people put aside their nearly-untouched plates.)*

RICK: Is everything okay?

WILLUM: Fine. Fine.

RICK: Okay.

CLELIA: Well.

WILLUM: So—uh, fill us in, Rick. What have you been doing these last —however many years it's been?

RICK: *(Who, we discover, is blessed with total recall.)* Oh. Okay—let's see. *(He rolls his eyes upward to help himself remember, and recounts in droning singsong.)* Nineteen seventy o-o-one, March, I g-e-et out of the Army, I go-o back to work at my old place where I used to work, the same factory, y'know—and, it's really pretty much the same as it was, you know? I mean, okay, there are some new things, okay, granted—but basically it's really, uh, the same. Pretty much. 'Kay, then, uh, in April, I mo-ove in with my brother at my brother's place 'cause he lives right near there, and I'm still—still workeen' at the factory. Okay. Uh, Ma-ay—

WALDGRAVE: Jesus.

RICK: Huh?

WALDGRAVE: Nothing.

RICK: 'Kay. May of 1971, I'm sti-i-ll workeen' at the factory—.

WILLUM: Uh, Rick—maybe—maybe you could give us, like, an *overview* of the whole time.

AXEL: For those of us who didn't bring our pajamas.

WILLUM: I mean, like—okay, what sort of job is it that you do, again? I remember your saying your factory made something interesting, but I —uh, what was it again?

RICK: Chalk.

WILLUM: *(Trying to find something fascinating in this revelation.)* Oh? Chalk?

RICK: Yeah. *(Shrugs.)* We make chalk.

WILLUM: Uh-huh? Uh-huh? And anything else? Or just—?

RICK: Just the chalk.

WILLUM: Just the chalk. Uh-huh? Well, so, what's your part in that process?

RICK: Inspector.

WILLUM: Yeah? So—uh, what does an inspector do?

RICK: *(Shrugs.)* Sit there and watch the chalk.

WILLUM: Uh-huh? Uh-huh?

RICK: The loaders put the chalk in the crates, then the crates come through, and I check 'em out.

WILLUM: And you—what is it that you look for? (RICK *looks puzzled.*) Is it—uh, color variations, or broken pieces, or what?

RICK: *(Shrugs.)* I just make sure there *is* some.

WILLUM: Some what?

RICK: Some chalk in the crates.

WILLUM: Oh! Oh, I see—so, what, is there sometimes no chalk in the crates?

RICK: There's always chalk in the crates. They're crates of chalk. We don't just send out some crates with no chalk. Why would we do that?

WILLUM: So—uh, what is it that you do?

RICK: What do I do? I make *sure* there's chalk in the crates.

WILLUM: Oh.

RICK: It sounds neat but it's really not. (RICK, *to everyone's dismay, takes another devilled egg.)*

WILLUM: So you still live with your brother?

RICK: My brother Bob, yeah. Him and his wife.

WILLUM: Big place?

RICK: Yeah. Couple of rooms, you know.

WILLUM: Oh!

RICK: Yeah. It's nice, though. They don't really come around that much, lately. Less and less.

WILLUM: Really? Where do they go?

RICK: *(Frowns slightly.)* I'm not sure. Takeen' the kids for a walk, stuff like that, I guess.

WILLUM: Kids? They've got kids?

RICK: Oh, yeah. Little Bob junior, and little Richard the third.

WILLUM: *(Laughing.)* Richard the third?

RICK: *(A trifle put off by* WILLUM*'s laughter.)* Yeah. My dad was Richard Steadman, and I'm Richard junior, really. It's a family name. Richard.

WILLUM: *(Still smiling.)* Makes sense.

RICK: It's not that unusual of a name in Wisconsin.

WILLUM: No, I'm sorry. Then—so, are you on vacation now, or what?

RICK: Yeah. And I was just gonna, you know, hang around the house, but my brother—I don't know how he did it, but he gave me all this money, like *mucho dinero,* y'know, and all these credit cards. And said why didn't I just go anywhere I wanted to? So that's what I'm doeen', just travelleen' around. . . .

WILLUM: Well, that was generous of him.

RICK: You know it. Especially since he hasn't got a job, or anything.

WILLUM: No?

RICK: No. He's on that welfare. He used to work at the chalk factory, but he got laid off.

WILLUM: Why?

RICK: Well, I came back from the army. They gave me my old job back.

WILLUM: Oh!

RICK: Yeah, they had to. That was the law. Too bad for old Bob, though.

WILLUM: Gee—well, I'm sure you help out with the household expenses, don't you?

RICK: *(Rubbing his nose.)* Oh . . . prob'ly.

WILLUM: Is, uh—is Bob okay about it all? I mean, is he happy with the situation?

RICK: Oh, sure. He has his interests, you know, like—oh, his headphones, and . . . and walkeen' down by the river . . . and tryeen' to find places to put things. And recently he's gotten interested in guns. . . . *(He tries to think of something else Bob enjoys.)*

AXEL: I'll bet.

RICK: Lots of stuff.

CLELIA: You were never married?

RICK: Aw, no. The only time I ever proposed was 'way back, I still remember, we were all out on the playground one time at Reever Hadley Elementary School, and we were playeen'—. *(He smiles shyly, which proves surprisingly, if momentarily, disarming.)* I don't think I ever told anybody this—.

CLELIA: *(With a mother's smile.)* What happened?

RICK: Aw, there was this real pretty little girl, you know. I'll never forget, her name was Tina Patsavas, and she—one day I gave her this little necklace that I made myself out of Cheerios—you know, you paint the Cheerios and you string 'em all together? (CLELIA *nods.*) I thought she'd like it; what did I know, right? So, I gave her that, and then I asked her if she'd marry me.

CLELIA: *(Genuinely touched.)* Ohhh. . . .

RICK: And she was real nice, but she said she couldn't. You know.

CLELIA: *(Smiling.)* Oh, how sad.

RICK: Then she told her folks, and they got all mad. It was pretty dumb of me, I guess.

CLELIA: Oh, it wasn't. It was very sweet.

RICK: You think?

CLELIA: Of *course* it was.

RICK: Really?

CLELIA: *Yes.*

RICK: I mean, what the heck, she was only about eight, or sometheen'.

CLELIA: And how old were you?

RICK: Thirty.

CLELIA: *(Horrified.)* Oh!

RICK: Boy, I wish I'd had you there to tell her folks that it was so sweet. They didn't think it was sweet, boy. They wanted to put me in *jail.*

CLELIA: Oh!

RICK: But no, that really makes me feel better, though, that you thought it was sweet. I have to remember that next time. (TANSY *enters with the spaghetti.*)

TANSY: Spaghetti!

CLELIA: *(Jumping up and whispering to* TANSY.) Tansy, could I—do you think I could have another—? *(She gestures toward the saucers.)*

TANSY: *(Whispering.)* Oh. Sure. (CLELIA *surreptitiously grabs a saucer and disappears into the kitchen.)*

WALDGRAVE: What was all that?

TANSY: *(Taking* RICK *the spaghetti.)* I think she just needed a little time alone.

WALDGRAVE: Oh.

RICK: Thanks. *(He eats a strand or two of spaghetti.)*

TANSY: Well, how were the devilled—*(She looks around, seeing the barely-tasted eggs lying here and there—not to mention the untouched entrees.)* eggs?

WILLUM: Uh—.

RICK: Great! As a matter of fact—*(Cute-regretfully.)* guess what?

TANSY: *(Not letting herself guess.)* What?

RICK: I'm full. *(He shrugs.)*

TANSY: *(Staying in control.)* Oh. . . ? Uh, well—you—you're full?

RICK: Yep.

TANSY: Uh—.

RICK: *(Giving her his plate of spaghetti.)* So, what do you want to do with this?

AXEL: *(To* TANSY.) Oh, go ahead!

WILLUM: Tansy! *(Going to her.)* Let me help—. *(He guides her toward the kitchen, whispering.)* He saved my life, Tansy.

TANSY: I know. I know that.

WILLUM: I can explain about the food.

TANSY: It doesn't matter. *(She takes the spaghetti into the kitchen.)*

RICK: Pop it in the warmer, I guess.

WILLUM: Tansy? Are you all right in there? (CLELIA *enters, barely acknowledges the others, picks up two more saucers, and hurries back to the kitchen. In a moment, we hear the violent smashing of crockery within.* TANSY *and* CLELIA *enter, looking refreshed.* TANSY *even wears an ESTful smile.)* What happened in there?

TANSY: Why, nothing.

WILLUM: I heard something.

TANSY: Just—girl talk.

WILLUM: Oh. . . .

RICK: *(After a small belch, he thumps his chest, smiles.)* Well! Excu-u-u-u-u-u-use me-e-e-e-e-e-e-e! *(He smiles again.)* Y'ever do that? Ever do impressions? See if you get this one—*(In a gruff voice, shaking his head violently.)* "I got a *milli*on of 'em! *I* got a *milli*on of 'em! Ha! Chachachachachacha!" *(He looks around.)* Jimmy Durante. Before he died. Okay, how about this, how about—

AXEL: *(In pain.)* Please—

RICK: *(In an adenoidal stammer.)* "Har-Har-Harvey—big, white-white-white-white rab-rab-rabbit."

AXEL: Not impressions—

RICK: *(Smiles.)* Jimmy Stewart. Okay?

AXEL: Anything but impressions—

RICK: Okay, let's see—. *(Shoulders up, head down, pointing with both hands.)* "*You-u-u-u-u-u-u! Dirty ra-a-a-a-a-at!*"

WALDGRAVE: I think we're going.

TANSY: Oh, no, wait—uh, *game time!*

AXEL: *(Recovering.)* Huh?

RICK: James Cagney!

TANSY: We're going to play a game, then we're going to cut the cake! *(To* WALDGRAVE.) It's Willum's birthday.

WALDGRAVE: Well—.

TANSY: All right, everyone, find a seat. You too, Ax. *(They do.)*

WILLUM: *(About to give up on the evening.)* Tansy—.

TANSY: Here we go, don't worry. We're going to play, "I Went On a Trip." *(To the* WALDGRAVES.) Have you ever played that?

WALDGRAVE: I'm not sure.

CLELIA: Oh, yes!

TANSY: The first person names something beginning with "A"—"I went on a trip, and I brought an apple," for instance.

RICK: Oh, right. I've played this.

TANSY: *(Relieved.)* Good! Then the next person adds something that starts with "B," and so on—and the list just keeps growing.

WALDGRAVE: Oh, yeah.

RICK: I've played this.

TANSY: Good. Good. All right, here we go. You want to start, Mr.—Ticky?

WALDGRAVE: All right. "I went on a trip, and I brought—an apple," what the hell.

TANSY: That's fine. And, Clelia?

CLELIA: *(Carefully.)* "I went on a trip and I brought an apple and—a basket."

TANSY: For the apples, right? *(There are polite chuckles.* CLELIA *smiles at her own cleverness.)* All right—Axel?

AXEL: *(Sullenly.)* "I went on a trip, and I brought an apple, a basket, and a cucumber."

TANSY: All right, let me see—"I went on a trip, and I brought an apple, a basket, a cucumber, and—a duck." *(She looks brightly to* RICK.)

RICK: 'Kay? Uh—"I went on a trip, and I brought an a-apple, a basket, a cucumber, and a duck, and—a map of the area." *(He looks to* WILLUM, *smiling.)*

TANSY: Uh, wait—.

AXEL: He loses, right?

TANSY: No, shh. Uh, Rick—

RICK: Huh?

TANSY: You can't—maybe I didn't explain this; see, you're supposed to say something beginning with "E."

RICK: Huh?

TANSY: Yeah—see, apple was with "A"—"B" was basket, "C" was cucumber, "D" was duck—

RICK: Oh.

TANSY: See?

RICK: *(To whom, apparently, this rule seems pointless.)* Oh, we never played that way. We always just—you know, we'd just name things we'd really take on a trip.

TANSY: Oh. . . .

RICK: Like a map of the area.

TANSY: Oh—well. . . .

RICK: So would that be okay?

TANSY: *(Looking to* WILLUM.) Well—?

WILLUM: Sure. Sure.

TANSY: *(To* RICK.) All right, sure. You—then why don't you do it your way, and we'll just keep going the way we were. *(To everyone else.)* All right? *(The others shrug their acquiescence.)*

RICK: *(To* WILLUM.) Your turn. Go.

WILLUM: Uh—what's my letter?

TANSY: "F." Pretend he did an "E."

WILLUM: Okay. Uh—"I went on a trip, and I brought an apple, a basket, a cucumber, a duck, a map of the area, and a—a flagpole."

RICK: A flagpole?

WILLUM: Yeah.

RICK: *(With a look at the others.)* On a trip? Okay. *(He shakes his head, looks down smiling.)*

TANSY: Ticky?

WALDGRAVE: Oh, boy. "I went on a trip, and I brought an apple, a basket, a cucumber, a duck, a map of the area, a flagpole, and a gun."

CLELIA: "I went on a trip, and I brought an apple, a basket, a cucum . . . ber. . . ." *(She stops, having noticed* RICK, *who is now writing in a pad.)*

TANSY: Rick? What—what are you doing?

RICK: *(Looking up.)* Maybe you guys can remember all these, but I sure can't. *(He finishes writing.)* Okay.

CLELIA: *(Uncertainly, as bewildered looks waft back and forth around her.)* "I went on a trip, and I brought a—an apple, and a—."

RICK: *(Consulting his list, prompting her in a whisper that would wake Jonestown.)* "A basket."

CLELIA: I know—but—but—.

WALDGRAVE: What're we—? What's the point of this, if—?

TANSY: Why don't we play something else?

WILLUM: Good idea.

WALDGRAVE: Or maybe we could just—.

RICK: All right, all right. Wait a minute. This is called "Shoes and Socks," all right? First, everybody take off your shoes and socks. *(The others glance uncertainly around.)* Come on. Everybody take off your shoes and socks.

WALDGRAVE: *(About to demur.)* Well—. *(He frowns at* CLELIA.)

RICK: Okay, what? You want me to go back? Or you understand everything so far?

WALDGRAVE: What?

RICK: You remember everything so far?

WALDGRAVE: What's to remember? All you said was, "Take off your shoes and socks."

RICK: Right, and, oh, we'll need some bags, some paper bags. *(To* WILLUM.) You got any paper bags?

WILLUM: Uh, Rick, now what are we doing, here?

RICK: "Shoes and Socks."

WILLUM: Yeah. . . ?

RICK: "Shoes and Socks," it's a game.

WILLUM: Oh.

RICK: It's fun, you'll see. Okay, so, uh, okay, so we need some bags. Some paper bags, one big one for the shoes and socks, and then some more for our heads.

CLELIA: For our—?

WALDGRAVE: *(Checking his watch.)* I don't know, it might be getting a little late.

RICK: You don't want to play this? I mean, we played *your* game, I mean, don't we wanna play *my* game?

WILLUM: *(Sudden decision.)* Sure. Fine, okay. Let's play it. *(Hopefully, to* WALDGRAVE.) It's really probably fun.

WALDGRAVE: *(Glowering a little at* WILLUM.) If you say so.

RICK: Okay, so take off your shoes and socks, and we need some bags, then.

TANSY: *(Going to the kitchen.)* Grocery bags all right?

RICK: That's great, that's great. Grocery bags. No groceries in 'em, though! Okay. So off with the shoes and socks. Or stockeen's, or whatever. *(Everyone—except* RICK—*begins following the instructions.)*

WALDGRAVE: I've been wearing these socks all day. They may be a little—Clelia! (CLELIA *is trying, as demurely as possible, to remove her stockings, but finding it hard to do so modestly.*)

CLELIA: *(Wincing.)* Well—?

WALDGRAVE: Stop that!

CLELIA: *(One shoe off, she hobbles to the kitchen.)* Uh, maybe I'd better do this in the kitchen.

WALDGRAVE: Good idea.

TANSY: *(Entering with bags.)* Paper bags!

RICK: Great!

CLELIA: Uh, Tansy—maybe you'd like to join me in here.

TANSY: What?

WILLUM: To take off your, uh—.

TANSY: Oh! Hey! Good thinkin'. *(She goes to the kitchen with* CLELIA.*)*

AXEL: Pretty exciting. Who'll be shirts and who'll be skins?

RICK: No, wait. Before that—.

AXEL: Be*fore* that?

RICK: *(Picking up a big bag with twine handles.)* Here, we can do this—.

WALDGRAVE: *(Holding up his footgear.)* What are we supposed to do with these?

RICK: Okay, these go, all go in a bi-ig bag. *(He starts roughly stuffing the bag with shoes and socks.)*

WALDGRAVE: Careful. Those shoes cost me a hundred bucks.

WILLUM: You mix 'em up?

RICK: *(Shaking the bag vigorously.)* Right, you're supposed to. Mix 'em up re-al good. . . .

AXEL: Allow to marinate, and serve hot.

RICK: No, wait. Okay. Now we take the other bags, everybody gets one—. (CLELIA *and* TANSY *reenter, shoes and stockings in hand.)* Oh, okay, here, just dump those in here. *(They obey.)* There you go. *(Shaking bag again.)* Mix, mix, mix. (WALDGRAVE *winces.)* Okay. And so you ta-ake your bag, right? And you—oh, yeah, you tear out one eye-hole, so you just see out of one eye. Everybody do that? *(Everybody starts tearing carefully.)*

WALDGRAVE: Mind telling us why we're doing this?

RICK: Otherwise you wouldn't be able to see.

AXEL: Right.

RICK: All torn out? Okay. Now pu-ut all the bags over your head, and look out of the eye. *(They do so, with varying success.)* 'Kay, now— uh, let's see—

WALDGRAVE: *(Having trouble aligning his eye-hole with his eye.)* Just— hold it a minute, dammit! Hell.

CLELIA: What is it, Ticky?

WALDGRAVE: I can't find the damned eye-hole. Gimme a hand, here.

RICK: I'll help you.

WALDGRAVE: My wife will help me!

CLELIA: I can't find you.

WALDGRAVE: I'm right here, dammit!

CLELIA: *(Touching* WILLUM*'s rear.)* There, is that you?

WILLUM: *(Politely.)* I think that's *me.*

CLELIA: Oh.

WALDGRAVE: I'm right here!

CLELIA: *(Finding WALDGRAVE.)* Here you are.

WALDGRAVE: Where's the eye-hole?

CLELIA: *(Trying to see.)* Well, hold still.

WALDGRAVE: I *am.*

CLELIA: *(Finding his eye-hole—almost amused.)* Well, Ticky? You made your eye-hole 'way too *high.*

WALDGRAVE: What?

CLELIA: *No*body's eye is 'way up there, sweetheart.

WALDGRAVE: How the hell am *I* supposed to know where it is? You think I punch out eye-holes for my goddam living?

CLELIA: *(Struggling with WALDGRAVE's paper bag.)* I really don't think —I can get this down far enough.

RICK: Here, no problem. We just poke a new one. *(He pokes WALD-GRAVE roughly in the eye with his finger, but fails to break the paper.)*

WALDGRAVE: *Ow!*

RICK: Here, wait—. *(He pokes him again, still without making a hole.)*

WALDGRAVE: *Ow!* God dammit!

RICK: One more time—.

WALDGRAVE: Get away from me! *(He swings wildly, hitting WILLUM in the stomach. WILLUM drops to his knees.)*

Patricia Kalember, Peter Riegert, Robert Joy and Mark Hamill

Wayne Tippit and Mark Hamill

Pamela Blair and Peter Riegert

Robert Joy and Mark Hamill

TANSY: Willum!

RICK: You okay?

WILLUM: *(Forcing a little laugh.)* Fine. Fine. *(He rises unsteadily.)*

WALDGRAVE: *(Talking to the fireplace.)* Who'd I hit?

WILLUM: It's all right.

WALDGRAVE: Willum? Was that you I hit?

WILLUM: No, it's okay, I'm fine.

WALDGRAVE: I say we can this game right now, before someone gets hurt.

TANSY: I second!

RICK: *(On the verge of being hurt.)* Well—it's really a good game.

WILLUM: Okay, then, no, let's—let's play the game. We'll just be careful.

WALDGRAVE: I don't want to play. I think my eye is swelling up in here.

WILLUM: Uh, Rick?

RICK: Well, I mean, we didn't even give it a chance, yet, y'know? I mean, not mentioning any names or anything, but somebody didn't even find his eye-hole yet.

WALDGRAVE: Why you—! *(He raises his hand to strike again.)*

CLELIA: Ticky! Please.

WILLUM: Yeah, please, Mr. Waldgrave, just as a favor to me. Okay?

CLELIA: Here. Here's what we'll do. We'll just open the side of your bag—*(She does so.)* and pull it down till you can—see. There. *(We can at last see* WALDGRAVE*'s angry, bloodshot eye peering from his eye-hole. We wish we couldn't.)* That should be all right, shouldn't it?

RICK: *(Surveying him.)* I don't know. It sure looks funny.

WALDGRAVE: Well goddammit, what the hell is this, a game or a goddam beauty contest!

CLELIA: *(Reproving.)* Ticky!

WALDGRAVE: Let's get the hell *on* with it!

RICK: Okay. Okay. Lemme see. *(Trying to remember.)* Okay, wait a minute. Okay—.

WALDGRAVE: Get on with it!

RICK: All right, so okay, ne-e-ext? Everybody has to close their eyes— their eye—and then turn all around and around till I say "Shoes and Socks" real loud. Okay, and I'm gonna hide the shoes and socks so-o-omewhere in the room, so—oh, and so put your fingers in your ears and hum, okay?

WALDGRAVE: I'm not doing this.

RICK: What, am I goeen' too fast again?

WILLUM: Please, Mr. Waldgrave—

WALDGRAVE: Put my fingers in my ears and turn around and hum! I own eight hotels! I come here to do a little business and maybe have a little drink, and *look* at me! I'm barefoot and half-blind with my goddam head in a bag! And now some goddam *chalk* inspector is standing here telling me to put my fingers in my ears and turn around and hum!

RICK: Right. Okay?

WALDGRAVE: No!

WILLUM: Please, Mr. Waldgrave—Ticky—.

WALDGRAVE: Mr. Waldgrave!

WILLUM: —Mr. Waldgrave—it'd mean a lot if we just got through this.

WALDGRAVE: Forget it, pal. I draw the line at humming.

WILLUM: *(Imploring.)* Rick—now, does everybody have to hum?

RICK: *(Shrugs.)* Well, sure. I don't make these rules, you know.

WALDGRAVE: I'm not humming.

WILLUM: Mr. Waldgrave—listen—if you could just play along this once, I'll make it up. I'll—listen, I'll take all that molding off the hotel.

WALDGRAVE: What?

TANSY: *(Trying to stop him.)* Willum—.

WILLUM: *(To* TANSY.) No, I think I've gotta do this. How about it, Mr. Waldgrave?

WALDGRAVE: You mean you'll get rid of all that old-fashioned junk?

WILLUM: Right.

WALDGRAVE: If I hum?

WILLUM: Yes.

AXEL: This how they built the Taj Mahal?

WALDGRAVE: *(Grimly.)* Okay. I'll hum.

TANSY: *(Heartsick at* WILLUM's *sacrifice.)* Oh, Willum. . . .

WILLUM: *(Brightly.)* Hey! Okay! *(Claps.)* Let's play "Shoes and Socks."

TANSY: Let's play "Taps."

RICK: All right, no, this first. Evrybody ready? Close your eyes and no peekeen'! Ready? A-a-aand—*go! (Everybody, bag on head, covers his ears and begins revolving and humming.* RICK *tiptoes about, looking for a place to hide the shoes and socks. It is during this bizarre procedure, naturally, that* THOR *decides to peek from his hiding place. The bedroom door opens, but just for a moment.)*

THOR: EEEEE! *(The door slams shut.)*

CLELIA: What was that?

WALDGRAVE: I don't know.

RICK: Keep hummeen'! Keep hummeen'!

WALDGRAVE: Look, don't push it, pal!

WILLUM: The Regency, Mr. Waldgrave! Think of the hotel! *(They go back to their routine.* RICK *finally rests the bag of shoes and socks on the sill of the open window, then pulls the shade down to cover them. He tiptoes quickly to another part of the room.)*

RICK: Okay! Stop! *(They stop, some with a little difficulty.)*

WALDGRAVE: "Stop," what's this "stop" business? I thought you were supposed to say, "Shoes and Socks."

RICK: Right, oh, right. 'Kay—"Shoes and Socks!"

WALDGRAVE: Well, we're *stopped now!*

RICK: 'Kay.

TANSY: *(Seeing* CLELIA *massaging an ankle.)* Are you all right?

CLELIA: *(In pain.)* Fine.

WALDGRAVE: So what now? Let's finish this.

RICK: 'Kay, now what happens—I'm gonna just start readeen' out loud from any point in the Bible, and when I come to just anything about shoes, or feet, or anything like that—or legs—then whoever hears it, yell "Shoes and Socks!"

WILLUM: Uh, Rick—.

RICK: Or, maybe not legs, maybe just feet. Okay?

WILLUM: Rick, wait. Now, what, we need a Bible?

RICK: Right—oh, yeah, right, we just—a Bible and we just open it up to anywhere—.

WILLUM: Rick, I—I don't think I have a Bible.

RICK: You don't have a Bible?

AXEL: What do you think this is, the Ramada?

WILLUM: I'm sorry, but I'm just sure I don't.

RICK: I thought *every*body has a Bible—don't they?

TANSY: Maybe it doesn't have to be a Bible. Maybe we could use something else—a dictionary, or a catalogue, or—.

RICK: *(Solemnly.)* No, it's gotta—

RICK, TANSY & WILLUM: —be a Bible.

WILLUM: Right.

RICK: Why don't you have a Bible? Don't you believe in God?

WILLUM: It isn't that I don't—Rick, this isn't a question that I'd like to get into with a bag over my head.

RICK: Well—*(Shrugs and sighs.)* that's that, then. *(He sits and selects an hors d'oeuvre.)*

WALDGRAVE: What? The game's over?

RICK: Sure. How would I know he wouldn't of had a Bible? *(People start removing their paper bags.)* It really kind of makes you think, you know?

WILLUM: What do you mean?

RICK: *(With solemn irony.)* I mean, if you'd believed in a power higher than yourself, we could've had a great game of "Shoes and Socks" here tonight.

WILLUM: *(Pained.)* Aw, Rick—.

RICK: *(Cocking his head to one side and raising an eyebrow.)* Doesn't this make you ask yourself—what *else* in life you might be misseen'?

WALDGRAVE: I'm missing my shoes and socks, do you mind?

RICK: Oh, right. *(Crosses to window.)* I forgot. Here we go. *(He releases the windowshade, and the bag of shoes and socks tumbles backwards into the darkness.)* Oop. *(We hear a faint splash. Regretting it but taking no blame.)* Sounds like they landed in some water.

WALDGRAVE: Aw—!

RICK: *(Referring to the sill.)* This is slanted, or sometheen'.

WALDGRAVE: *(Barging out the door.)* Aw, for the love o' Pete—!

CLELIA: *(Following him.)* Ticky—! *(She leaves, limping down the stairs. AXEL follows her out, lighting a cigarette, to observe the search from the porch. We hear WALDGRAVE cussing and splashing below.)*

RICK: *(Also on his way out, he turns back to WILLUM. Tilting his head to one side again and smiling with only his upper lip.)* Awww—let's see that old smile, hey? We forgive you. *(He exits and descends the stairs.)*

WILLUM: *(As if trying to awake from a bad dream.)* Aaaaaah!

TANSY: *(Coming to him.)* Oh, Willum.

WILLUM: *(In a hoarse whisper.)* He forgives me! Rick for*gives* me! What have I *done?*

TANSY: Don't listen to him.

WILLUM: He thinks I'm some kind of—godless—party-pooper. Is that what I am? A godless party-pooper?

TANSY: What you are is a good guy—and you're paying for it.

WILLUM: If I'm so good, why do I feel so bad?

TANSY: You should've told him to take a hike.

WILLUM: I owe him my life!

TANSY: *(Hugging him.)* I know.

WALDGRAVE'S VOICE: *(From outside and below.)* Gimme me a hand, here!

RICK'S VOICE: Grab my arm! *(Pause.)* Oop!

WALDGRAVE'S VOICE: Aaah! *(We hear a prolonged splash. On the porch,* AXEL *blows a perfect smoke ring.)*

WILLUM: *(Having listened impotently to the exchange outside, he turns imploringly to* TANSY.) Please don't leave me, Tansy!

TANSY: *(Saying this always hurts.)* I just gotta. I've gotta go to Washington.

WILLUM: Tonight?

TANSY: No, not tonight.

WILLUM: Oh, I just meant—,

TANSY & WILLUM: —tonight.

TANSY: Oh.

WILLUM: *(Ashamed.)* I'm sorry.

TANSY: Oh, don't be sorry. I know how you're feeling. But I can't, baby. Not tonight.

WILLUM: Tansy—.

TANSY: If I stay tonight, I'm afraid I'd never leave.

WILLUM: *(Frustrated.)* Uh—.

TANSY: I can't talk about this anymore, Willum. *(She exits quickly and goes down the stairs. Maddened,* WILLUM's *gaze fixes on the monster-head on the end-table. Unable longer to bear its sight, he snatches it up, throws open the bedroom door, and flings the head angrily inside.)*

THOR: *(Offstage.)* EEEEEEEEEEE! (THOR *bolts in terror from the bedroom, seeking asylum anywhere. He pulls open the closet door, only to be confronted with the flopping, headless monster costume hanging thereon.)* EEEEEEEE! *(He faints.)*

WILLUM: Thor! Oh, no! *(He rushes to the limp form of the boy, trying to revive him with slaps on the cheek.)* Please, Thor, wake up! Don't do this to me, Thor! *(We hear the others ascending the stairs outside.)* I'll give you two hundred dollars, Thor! Wake up! *(No response.)* Aaaah! *(On a desperate impulse,* WILLUM *piles* THOR's *body into the closet and closes the door. And just in time, for in comes the group, minus* RICK. WALDGRAVE *is the worst for wear, having been the rescuer of the shoes and socks. One side of him is wet up to the hip. Leaves, mud, possibly even a salamander, cling to him. His eye is worse. In his arms is a heavy, dripping tangle of stockings, shoes, socks, leaves, and decomposing grocery bag.* TANSY *is assisting* CLELIA, *who is now limping noticeably, and who has somehow acquired a little scratch on her forehead.* WILLUM, *not exactly at his best, claps his hand to his head and a sharp, panicky bark of laughter erupts from him unbidden.)* Oh, wow!

WALDGRAVE: *(Fixing him with an excoriating look.)* Yeah. "Oh, wow." (WALDGRAVE *dumps the mess in the middle of the floor.)*

WILLUM: *(After a furtive glance toward the closet.)* Uh, maybe we'd like to do this in the kitchen, like in the sink? *(No response from* WALD-

GRAVE, *who is doggedly untangling the sopping footwear. Just as brightly.)* Or maybe right here on the rug, this'd be fine, too.

WALDGRAVE: *(Handing a pair of mud-covered shoes to* CLELIA.) Here, these yours?

CLELIA: I'm not sure. I think—no.

AXEL: *(Looking at them closely.)* No, those are mine. *(He takes them and holds them gingerly aloft.)*

WALDGRAVE: These?

CLELIA: Yes. Thank you.

WILLUM: We can wash off in the kitchen, want to?

WALDGRAVE: *(Ignoring him, he pulls out a stocking.)* Stockings?

AXEL: Mine. (WALDGRAVE *looks at him.)* Kidding.

CLELIA: They may be mine.

TANSY: Yes.

WALDGRAVE: Here's a couple stuck together.

TANSY: It's called pantyhose. *(Grabbing them quickly.)* Thank you.

WALDGRAVE: *(To* WILLUM.) Here, these yours?

WILLUM: No, they're not.

WALDGRAVE: They gotta be.

WILLUM: They're really not.

CLELIA: Wait a minute. These aren't mine.

WILLUM: Those are mine.

CLELIA: So these are mine.

AXEL: Grab that gal and dance in line! *(Clapping in rhythm.)* Alaman left, say, "Ain't that fine!"

TANSY: Axel!

AXEL: Sorry.

WALDGRAVE: *(To* WILLUM, *as he stands, holding up his own pair of ruined shoes.)* Okay, pal. Hundred bucks, right? A hundred bucks it cost me, and maybe an eye, because we just had to play your old army buddy's little game. Okay. Before we go, you got any more little surprises for us? *(The closet door swings open, and out, with a small clunk, falls* THOR's *tiny arm.)*

CLELIA: Thor! *(She runs to retrieve him from the closet.)* Thor, baby!

WALDGRAVE: *(At the same time.)* Thor! *(To* WILLUM.*)* What the hell is this?

WILLUM: *(Too rattled to lie.)* He's all right, he's—he just fainted.

CLELIA: Fainted!

WALDGRAVE: *(To* WILLUM.*)* You saw this happen?

WILLUM: Yeah, right here, so—.

WALDGRAVE: He *fainted!*

WILLUM: Right.

WALDGRAVE: So you put him in the *closet?*

WILLUM: Well—.

WALDGRAVE: *Why?* Why would you *do* that?

WILLUM: *(Weakly.)* Well, he—he looked like that's where he was headed. (WALDGRAVE *now has the half-conscious* THOR *in his arms, and looks for all the world like the father of the drowned girl in Frankenstein.)*

WALDGRAVE: I don't believe this!

CLELIA: Thor—.

WALDGRAVE: Get our coats! (TANSY *goes for the coats.)*

CLELIA: Thor, can you hear me?

THOR: *(Faintly, after a pause.)* Who am I? *Where* am I?

AXEL: Oh, give us a break, Thor.

THOR: Dad!

WALDGRAVE: Son!

CLELIA: Thor!

THOR: Mom! (CLELIA *hugs* THOR.)

AXEL: John! Marsha! Pancho! Ceesco! *(Falsetto.)* Minnie! Mickey! *(Gathering his coat, etc.)* Happy ending! Look—Rinty's laughing too! *(He barks joyfully several times, and is gone.* TANSY *has brought the coats, which* CLELIA *accepts.)*

WALDGRAVE: Has everybody around here gone nuts?

TANSY: *(Handing* CLELIA *a stack of saucers.)* Here, Clelia, take these.

CLELIA: Oh, *thank* you—one will be fine. *(She puts the saucer in her purse.)*

WALDGRAVE: *(Stares at* CLELIA, *decides not to ask.)* We're getting outta here right now. *(To* WILLUM.) I'll see you in the morning, pal!

CLELIA: *(Remembering her manners, she speaks for the damaged, limping trio.)* Thank you so much. We had a very nice time.

WALDGRAVE: Clelia!

CLELIA: Well—? *(They clatter down the stairs.)*

TANSY: *(Her eyes welling with sympathy.)* I'd better go, too, Willum. *(She has picked up her purse.)*

WILLUM: *(Imploring.)* Oh, please don't go? *Please?*

TANSY: *(Wavering in her resolve.)* Well. . . . *(She starts to put her purse down.)*

RICK: *(Entering with suitcases, on one of which is pasted a happy-face.)* So where do I sleep?

TANSY: *(Picking up her purse again.)* Good night, Willum. *(To* RICK.*)* Good night. *(She leaves.)*

RICK: The couch okay? (WILLUM *can no longer speak.)* The couch? I mean, don't 'cause that's fine by me. *(Whatever that means. He starts unpacking.)* I spent, like, *mucho* time on these couches, believe me. Over to my brother's I slept on one two years one time. *(A door softly closes.* WILLUM *has gone into the bedroom.)* Hey. One tired guy. *(He gets comfortable on the couch, takes a music book and a tambourine from his suitcase, and props the open book on the coffee table—anchoring it, if need be, with an unused game hen. Then, studying the book, he begins to sing—starting, for some reason, at much too high a pitch.)*
"Oh-oh, say, can you seee—"
(He strikes the tambourine.)
"Through the dawn's early light—"
(Tambourine.)
"What so proud-ly we hailed
At the twilight's last gleameen'—"
(Tambourine. The bedroom door has opened just an inch or two, and beyond it we can see WILLUM*'s face, as he dully watches his new house guest grace the autumn night with song.* RICK *turns the page, fairly screaming to reach the notes.)*
"And the rock-ETS' RED GLARE!
The bombs burst-EEN' IN AIR. . . !"
(The lights fade.)

ACT TWO

ACT II

SCENE 1

We hear a hot 1920's foxtrot as the lights come up on the room, back to normal, a few days later. On the Right side of the coffee table are pencils, pens, watercolors, a drawing-board, masking tape, and illustration board, all recently set in order by Tansy. At present, shoeless, she lounges in an armchair, reading want-ads in the Washington Post. *Axel, looking sour, stands next to Willum's stereo, auditioning the record whose music we hear. It ends and rejects.*

AXEL: I can't figure it. He buys a seven-hundred-dollar stereo system, then the only records he plays on it are sixty years old and chiseled out of granite.

TANSY: Ax, don't you realize? That's one of the things that have kept the three of us together. We're old-fashioned. All of us, in different ways.

AXEL: Oh?

TANSY: Sure. Look at us. Willum with his records—me with my quaint little notions that you chide me for, about "gumption," and so on. And you—you know, there's another word you don't hear much these days—"curmudgeon." You, Ax, are a classic curmudgeon.

AXEL: "A classic curmudgeon"—sounds like a murder weapon.

TANSY: And listen to the way we talk—the way we all use outdated slang, have you noticed that?

AXEL: Aw, tie that bull outside. That's a bunch of malarkey. *(He reads a headline from the back of* TANSY's *paper.)* "Surprising Giants Shut Down Atlanta." *(A little alarmed.)* I hope that's the sports section.

TANSY: It is, yes. *(We hear an automobile outside.)*

AXEL: Who comes here?

TANSY: Is it both of them?

AXEL: *(At the window.)* No—his lordship's alone, for once.

TANSY: Wonder how he managed.

AXEL: Maybe he finally took my advice and showed Rick the river from the roof of the Mercantile Exchange. (WILLUM, *having thudded up the stairs, enters wearily. He is, beneath his exhaustion, a trifle wild-eyed. A portfolio is under one arm, and he drops it on the table.)*

TANSY: Hey, Cutie, how's it goin'? (WILLUM, *whom nobody else would have called "Cutie," forces a little smile but seems unable to speak.)*

AXEL: Where's the Amityville Horror? Still around? (WILLUM *shrugs.)* You don't want to talk about it? (WILLUM *touches his nose, the charades signal for "You guessed it." He takes out his "beeper," pushes a button, and listens as he loosens his tie.)*

WILLUM'S VOICE: This is Willum, November tenth. Leave any messages for me—or for Rick Steadman—as soon as you hear the tone. Thanks. *(The tone sounds.)*

RED GRAHAM'S VOICE: Hey, Boy. This is Red Graham again; now by this time I realize you're not just achin' to do this Alexandria job, but now let me try this out on you. S'pose I was to offer you—. (RED's *voice cuts off abruptly, and we hear the thunder of a microphone being blown into. Then several percussive taps. Then—)*

RICK'S VOICE: Testeen' one, two, three, four. One, two, three, four. Seems to be workeen' fine. *("Click.")*

RED GRAHAM'S VOICE: —that's my new unlisted number, and you can call me there anytime. 'Preciate it. So long. *(Tone sounds.)*

WALDGRAVE'S VOICE: Hello, this is Waldgrave; look, can you do me one thing as soon as you get in? There's a company in Lincoln, Neb—*(Again, the tape is interrupted.)*

RICK'S VOICE: *(After a tambourine sounds.)* 'Kay, it's the Ri-i-i-ick *Stead*man Show! *(Tambourine sounds again.)* Okay. Uh—. Wait a minute. 'Kay, the Rick *Stead*man Show, and today, for today's show, uh—for—the—uh, today's special guest, for to*day*—uh—(WILLUM *has blindly made his way to the bottle of Jack Daniel's, which he shakily tries to pour into a glass.)* is—goeen'—to—bee—Willum the Dopey Duck! Okay? Hey. *(Tambourine.* WILLUM *gives up trying to pour, drinks directly from the bottle. Then, bottle still in hand, he trudges, mesmerized, toward the machine.)* Hi, Willum. *(Sounding exactly the same.)* Hi, Rick. *(As the host again.)* Hi. So, um, tell us, Willum, first of all—how* are *you? (As* WILLUM *the Duck.)* Oh . . . *(A very long pause.)* fine . . . (WILLUM *turns off the volume, sits. Nobody speaks for some time.)*

WILLUM: *(Finally.)* Six days. Has it been just six days? To think—only a week ago, the day before my birthday *(He gives a sad little laugh.)* Tansy was leaving, the hotel design was being rejected and rejected . . . I found out I was being audited by the IRS—and in my folly I imagined myself unhappy. *(He takes another slug.)* He . . . he follows me. He seems to have unlimited time, unlimited funds—brother Bob's life savings, I guess—he takes an interest in my work, he goes with me into town. The other day—I'm not sure I can even talk about this yet—the other day, I had to take a commuter flight to St. Louis—that's where they're building the outside elevator for the Regency—and Rick wanted to come along. So I said, well, okay, it won't be much fun, but—. So, Rick came along. Everything's fine, he's sitting next to me on the plane, a DC-8, I think. He's wearing a little pilot's hat he bought at the airport; he's leafing through a bound copy of *Redbook*. Then suddenly—suddenly the plane starts shaking, the safety-belt lights come on—people are in fact starting to get alarmed. So what happens in the middle of this? Rick jumps up, stands in the middle of the aisle, and shouts . . . *(Finding it difficult to say.)* and shouts—"Urinate! . . . Urinate, or your kidneys will explode!" Honest to God. And I think—I mean I'm really pretty sure —some people *did*. I mean, he was wearing this dumb little pilot's hat, and that white shirt and tie he always wears. And, you know, in a panic situation like that—. Anyway, naturally, the next thing we hear is the pilot saying, "We experienced a little turbulence back there but we're out of it now, and we'll be landing in St. Louis in one minute." And Rick just sat down again, with no idea how many of those people wanted to murder him. I think he only escaped because the ones who really had the grounds didn't want to stand up.

TANSY: Unbelievable.

WILLUM: It's a hundred things a day like that. Little things mostly, but they're starting to take their toll. I'm becoming irrational, snappish—. I lie awake. After the shoes-and-socks party, it took me two days to square things with Waldgrave; and by then I was such an exhausted, cowering wreck at work—I've just been agreeing to everything; look at this. *(He takes a rendering from the portfolio.)*

AXEL: What's this?

WILLUM: That's the Regency. As of this morning.

TANSY: Pretty stark.

AXEL: Looks like a huge air conditioner.

WILLUM: I know, I know. I—well, I just keep telling myself, no matter how it ends up, it's still mine. It still has my name on it. And that's—something, I guess.

AXEL: I guess.

TANSY: Look—if this Rick person is ruining your career and your life, you have to do something about it, that's all.

WILLUM: I can't. I can't hurt his feelings. I owe him too much.

AXEL: Well, maybe he'll just drift away one of these days.

WILLUM: I don't think so. He's been dropping hints about what he'd like for Christmas.

TANSY: Oh, no.

AXEL: What does he want?

WILLUM: A "Mister Microphone."

AXEL: All right—something's obviously got to be done. What are the rules? We can't hurt his feelings, right?

WILLUM: That's right.

AXEL: All right, that makes it a little tricky. Here's one idea. See what you think of this. All right—you know when you travel, you spend time in a foreign country? I mean, it's fun, but it also puts a hell of a *strain* on you. I mean, people are talking different, they've got different customs, they all remember different things than you do. They eat weird things. Pretty soon you're glad to get back home. And the more bizarre the place is, the faster you get homesick.

WILLUM: So?

AXEL: So—just an idea—but I'm thinking, why couldn't we hit Rick with a dose of culture shock? I mean, what if we start confronting him with some rituals, and memories, and traditions he's never seen before?

WILLUM: *(Skeptical.)* Ax, how do we know what rituals and traditions Rick's never seen before?

AXEL: We make them up.

WILLUM: Oh, Ax.

AXEL: Really. I think we could do it.

WILLUM: What, in other words, leave him out.

AXEL: No, invite him to join in. If he gets fed up with us—hey! I bet if we could find things to do that are stupid enough, or strange, or boring enough—I betcha money Rick'll be on the next Amtrak back to Silverheels. What do you think?

WILLUM: I think that sounds really cowardly.

AXEL: I thought you'd like it. When do we rehearse?

WILLUM: We're not *going* to rehearse.

AXEL: *(Taking him by the shoulders.)* Willum, *face* it. This is a desperate situation. It calls for something infantile. (WILLUM *sighs.*) Kemp —that's who I bet could help us. Kemp would know some strange customs. He lives in a transient hotel in Indianapolis.

WILLUM: Ax—.

AXEL: *(Getting more excited.)* Oh, let me work on this; it could be—it could be that favor Tansy's always bugging me about.

WILLUM: What?

AXEL: Tansy's always saying, "Do somebody an anonymous favor, will you?" Well—this could be it. Of course, there's no way for it to be anonymous, but—.

TANSY: *(Astonished.)* Well, Axel—?

AXEL: What?

TANSY: Just—surprised you remembered that.

AXEL: So would this count with you? I mean, if Rick were to leave—?

TANSY: Well—it's not for me to say—.

AXEL: But?

TANSY: But—yes, all right; if you really somehow got Rick to leave Willum in peace, with no hard feelings—yes, in my book, that would count.

WILLUM: *(Setting up his drawing materials.)* Look—far be it from me to be a godless party-pooper, but you're going to have to forget this.

AXEL: Leave it for now. Call me if you change your mind. *(At the door.)* "Mister Microphone," huh? Wonder what he'll ask you for *next* Christmas? *(He leaves.)*

WILLUM: Oh, me.

TANSY: I'll go down, too. I've got phoning to do. *(She starts out with her paper.)*

WILLUM: What's that? Washington paper?

TANSY: The *Post*, yes. (WILLUM *smiles briefly, starts taping a piece of sketch paper to his drawing board.*) I—listen, for what it's worth—since this Rick thing started, I feel like a real traitor—.

WILLUM: No, pooh.

TANSY: I do. Leaving here Friday? Leaving you here, with him?

WILLUM: No, listen, I'm gonna say something to him. I will.

TANSY: Good.

WILLUM: I don't know what.

TANSY: *(At the window.)* Here he comes, he's walking down the road. You want me to stay?

WILLUM: I'll be fine. I'm doing my work.

TANSY: All right. *(She leaves.* WILLUM *starts to set up his drawing materials, then starts pacing back and forth in front of the couch, speaking objectively, maturely, to an imaginary* RICK.)

WILLUM: Now, Rick. Rick, sit down. *(Pause.)* Put down your tambourine. Now, as you know, there's a kind of—chemistry between any two people, which can affect both people in very different ways. Now, just as there's some chemistry in you which allows you to like my company—there's some chemistry in me that just always makes me want to scratch your face off. *(Abandoning that.)* No, um—*(Trying again—the no-nonsense approach.)* Rick, I'm not going to mince words. It's time for you to leave. We needn't go into all the reasons; let's just say it's something I've thought about and have decided on. Now, I realize that you saved my life. I owe you my life. I acknowledge that. And I realize that I promised—promised in writing—that as long as I was alive, you could come to me for anything, and that you would always have a place that you could—. *(Breaking off again.)* Oh, God. *(He picks up a large T-square.)* Rick, do you know what this is? This is a crossbow. *(Dispatching the imaginary* RICK *with an arrow.)* Thhhkkk! *(Turning the T-square on himself.)* Thhhkkk! *(He drops, slain, to the sofa. Presently he opens his eyes again.)* Oh, me. Oh, well. *(Getting back to work.)* Okay. Concentrate. If I just—

concentrate. (WILLUM *works, clenching a pencil far back in his teeth like a bit. Momentarily, in comes* RICK, *hands in pockets, head to one side—in a word, depressed. He sighs.* WILLUM *works. He sighs again, more loudly.* WILLUM *looks up grimly, the pencil still clenched in his teeth.)*

RICK: What are *you* smileen' about? (WILLUM *takes the pencil from his mouth, goes back to work.)* I'm not smileen'. 'Cause you wanta know *why? (No answer.)* Huh? *(No answer.)* You wanta know *why* I'm not smileen'? *(No answer.)* Huh?

WILLUM: *(Stopping work.)* All right. What's the problem?

RICK: You really want to know?

WILLUM: Sure.

RICK: Really?

WILLUM: Rick.

RICK: *(Sighs.)* Well—you know my brother Bob?

WILLUM: Brother Bob, yes.

RICK: I called him up this morneen', and you know what?

WILLUM: What?

RICK: He moved.

WILLUM: He—he *moved?*

RICK: Yep.

WILLUM: Moved where?

RICK: That was the thing. He didn't leave any forwardeen' address. It was so strange.

WILLUM: *(Hoping he is right.)* Well, surely—if he really has moved, surely he'll get in touch.

RICK: I don't know. I hope he at least sends my things.

WILLUM: Your things? What things?

RICK: My clothes? My chemistry set?

WILLUM: Uh—.

RICK: My chihuahua?

WILLUM: Your chi*hua*hua?

RICK: Yeah. Oh, you should see him. He's really lifelike.

WILLUM: Rick, wait. Where—where would Bob send your things?

RICK: *(Shrugs.)* Here, right?

WILLUM: Uh—here?

RICK: This is where I am, right?

WILLUM: Rick—? *(He tries to go on, but can only manage to repeat.)* Rick—?

RICK: *(Giving him his full attention.)* What?

WILLUM: Rick—there's something I have to say. (RICK *watches him with his all-purpose expression.)* All right. Here goes. Now—you're here. And I'm here. *(Stalling to think.)* Um . . . okay. Are you with me so far?

RICK: I'm a little bit lost.

WILLUM: Rick, all I said was, "You're here and I'm here."

RICK: Oh.

WILLUM: *(Exhales audibly.)* All right. Now—when—when two people are together a lot of the time, they can't help influencing each other, and influencing each other's ability to function. You—are you still with me?

RICK: *(Nods.)* You're here and I'm here.

WILLUM: *(Uncertainly.)* Rrright. *(Should he go back? He decides to press on.)* So. What we're talking about, really, is personality, isn't it? Uh—*(Telling a joke on himself.)* I mean, I know there are qualities in me that make it hard for some people to have me around—I'm sloppy, I lose things, I'm always getting lost. Some people aren't able to deal with that; it's not their fault, it's not my fault, it's just—personality. You see what I'm driving at? (RICK *gives a more-or-less affirmative shrug.)* Okay . . . So, we all have these character traits. So, what if, just out of curiosity—*(Trying to sound hypothetical.)* what if somebody were to say to you—oh—"Get out of here and don't ever come back"—something like that. I mean, I know it's hard, but if you stood back, do you think you could see what might lead a person to say that to you?

RICK: Oh, sure.

WILLUM: *Really?*

RICK: Oh, sure.

WILLUM: Oh, Rick. That's great.

RICK: Sure. Like if he hated me because I believed in God?

WILLUM: Oh, Rick.

RICK: Or believed in God, or—*(Getting into it like a game.)* or maybe he hates people 'cause they work in a factory?

WILLUM: *(A quiet moan.)* Ahhhhh. . . .

RICK: And he hates me because my hands are all rough, and stained with honest chalk? Y'know?

WILLUM: Rick. No. No decent person would hate you for—.

RICK: Or, what else? Oh! *(The best yet.)* How 'bout because I was in the war? And this guy hates people with purple hearts?

WILLUM: Oh, God.

RICK: What?

WILLUM: Nothing. Nothing. All right, just—let me ask you this. What would you say are the main differences between you—and me?

RICK: *(Shrugs.)* None.

WILLUM: None? You mean you and I are—are—?

RICK: The same. Sure. (WILLUM *looks at him a long moment, then picks up his T-square.)*

WILLUM: Rick, do you know what this is? (RICK *shrugs.* WILLUM *gives up both his campaign and his fantasy.)* It's a T-square. I've got to get back to work.

RICK: 'Kay. That was fun.

WILLUM: *(Shakily lighting a cigarette.)* Great.

RICK: You smoke cigarettes?

WILLUM: Yeah.

RICK: Since when?

WILLUM: Since the airport. *(He is searching for something.)*

RICK: Oh, that reminds me, hey. I bet you don't think I don't know what you're lookeen' for, right?

WILLUM: What?

RICK: Right?

WILLUM: What?

RICK: *(Who suddenly is in high spirits.)* Wait, don't even answer that.

WILLUM: Answer what?

RICK: Or—you wanna guess?

WILLUM: Guess *what?*

RICK: Huh?

WILLUM: Guess *what?*

RICK: I give up. (RICK *waits expectantly.* WILLUM *slumps into a chair. It would not surprise us to see him crumble into dust.)* What? Anything? Okay. I got one for *you.* You know your picture of that hotel?

WILLUM: *(Suddenly alert.)* That's what I was *look*ing for.

RICK: I know, 'cause you said you were afraid it was like *miss*een' sometheen', right?

WILLUM: I may have; Rick, if you've seen that—that's my final color rendering—.

RICK: No, I know, so this morneen' I to-o-ook it out, and I he-e-eld it up to the light—.

WILLUM: *(Barely audible.)* Rick—.

RICK: And I loo-o-ooked at it this way awhile, then I looked at it that way, then this way again—.

WILLUM: Rick, don't tell me you—.

RICK: No, wait. So guess what? You know what I finally realized it needed? So simple. *(He pulls the rendering from beneath the couch.)* A chimney! *(Imposed on the roof of a careful watercolor of the Regency is an immense, hideous, black square, boldly executed in some less refined medium—Crayola, perhaps, or laundry-marker. A second* square, on the opposite side of the roof, has been begun, then cancelled with a large "X." RICK points to the crossed-out mistake.) Not this one. That was just a goof. (He puts his hand over it.) But see?

WILLUM: Uh . . . Rick. . . ?

RICK: I don't know where I got the idea.

WILLUM: Rick—.

RICK: God, I guess.

WILLUM: (Looking closer, hoping that the drawing can somehow be saved.) Rick, you—did you put a hole in this?

RICK: Oh, right, that's why I remembered. Here, look. (He takes WILLUM's burning cigarette from the ashtray, gets a mouthful of smoke, and blows it slowly through the chimney-hole from behind. The effect is made a little surreal by the presence of RICK's eyes, which peer expectantly over the top of the drawing during the demonstration.) See? (He snorts happily.) Y'know, I thought I was a lot of things, but I sure never knew I was an architect!

WILLUM: (Who really doesn't.) Rick—I—I don't know what to say—.

RICK: That's okay. But, so—what would I do next, if I were—me?

WILLUM: (Clutching a pencil-box.) What?

RICK: I mean, you know, in the architect business. Could you like show me the ropes, and introduce me around, and that?

WILLUM: Uh—.

RICK: Or, wait a minute! Hey! We could be partners! (The box in WILLUM's hand suddenly shatters, crushed by his clenched fist. He grabs his wrist, pained.)

WILLUM: Aah!

RICK: (Running to him.) What happened?

WILLUM: *(Nursing his hand.)* Nothing, it's—.

RICK: Hey, you're *bleed*een'! *(Grabbing the wounded hand.)* Lemme look at that.

WILLUM: Ow!

RICK: You sit there, I know just the thing for that.

WILLUM: I'll take care of it.

RICK: Sit *there.* This is my mom's kitchen remedy, you just rub it into the cut.

WILLUM: Rick—I'm—don't.

RICK: Sit *there,* now—and don't *move.* I'll be in here heateen' up the salt! *(He disappears into the kitchen.)*

WILLUM: Heating up—? (WILLUM *starts for the bedroom, stops, looks back at the phone, then toward the kitchen, then the bedroom, then toward the phone again. Deciding, he rushes to it and furtively and clumsily punches out a number. We hear a ring, then* AXEL's *voice.)*

AXEL'S VOICE: Yeah?

WILLUM: Ax?

AXEL'S VOICE: Hey, babe.

WILLUM: When do we rehearse?

AXEL'S VOICE: How about tonight?

WILLUM: How about tonight. *(The lights fade.)*

ACT II

SCENE 2

In the dark, the light on the answering machine pulses red, and we hear recorded voices.

WILLUM'S VOICE: Hello, hello. This is Willum, November eleventh. If you have a message, you can leave it when you hear the tone. Thanks. *(Tone sounds.)*

RED'S VOICE: Mornin', son! This' Red. Now, I'm—I wouldn't want you to think I was callin' for any reason; naw, I just like gettin' on your tape every mornin', you know—that an' a little o.j. is what it takes to get me started these days. All righty. I'll call you again first thing tomorrow. Have a good one. Bye-bye. *(Tone sounds.)*

WALDGRAVE'S VOICE: Cubbert? Waldgrave. I just personally called your draftsman for a floor plan, he says he can't work without specifications. Nobody around here has seen you for days. Where the hell *are* you? And what are you *doing*?

DEAN'S VOICE: Hey, Will-o—Dean the Bean, here. Hey, I still got your checkbook. You want it? *(Lights come up on the room. It is early evening, November 11. On the upper level, a dinner table has been set up.* TANSY *enters from the kitchen, a trifle behind schedule, busily unfolding a white tablecloth. We notice that she's mouthing something, as if trying to recall something lengthy and freshly-learned.)*

KEMP'S VOICE: *(From the answering machine.)* Anything I can help you with?

TANSY: *(Startled.)* Oh! Kemp. I forgot you were still on.

KEMP'S VOICE: Always on, Miss McGinnis, always on.

TANSY: Uh-huh. *(She straightens the cloth, surveys the room.)* By the way, in case nobody bothers to thank you for all your help last night —however this hare-brained thing turns out—thanks.

KEMP'S VOICE: My pleasure. Tell me, Miss McGinnis—.

TANSY: Yes?

KEMP'S VOICE: What do you look like?

TANSY: Oh—what would you guess I looked like?

KEMP'S VOICE: Well—going just by the voice, of course—are you very small, do you live in a tree, and are you inordinately fond of nuts?

TANSY: *(Stops working.)* Look, you—I can pull your plug, you know.

KEMP'S VOICE: *(In mock ecstasy.)* Oh, God, oh, God!

TANSY: *(Laughing.)* Stop. (AXEL, *in a tux, enters the front door.)*

AXEL: How're we doing?

TANSY: *(Seeing the tux.)* Well, what's *this?*

AXEL: I may not get a chance to change. Later tonight, Kemp and I— Kemp? Are you still with us?

KEMP'S VOICE: Sir.

AXEL: We're going to the dedication of the new Terre Haute Arts Pavilion.

TANSY: "Arts Pavilion"?

KEMP'S VOICE: Yes. It's quite beautiful, they say. It's built entirely out of creosote.

AXEL: Yes. . . . *(There is a sound from the porch.)* Who's this, is this our boy?

TANSY: Let's hope. (WILLUM *enters. His wounded hand is bound in fresh bandage.)*

WILLUM: Sorry I'm late. They were so backed-up at the clinic, I thought they'd never get to me. *(Holds up his hand.)* But they did, finally.

AXEL: Did they get out all the salt?

WILLUM: Most of it.

TANSY: That's good.

AXEL: Kemp is with us again—I suspect to give us his St. Crispin's-Day speech.

WILLUM: Oh. Hi, Kemp.

KEMP'S VOICE: Hello. Forgive me for not rising.

WILLUM: *(Nervous, and oblivious to wit.)* That's okay. So—Rick's not here? His car's outside.

TANSY: Not yet.

AXEL: Did you get things set up?

WILLUM: Hunh? Oh, yeah. I told him we were having a traditional Terre Haute dinner.

AXEL: Good.

WILLUM: *(Still on edge, to* TANSY.) And you're—you're making, uh—? You're making—uh—?

AXEL: Whoopee?

WILLUM: What? No—.

AXEL: Making tracks? Making do?

WILLUM: No—.

AXEL: Making out? Making believe? This is kind of fun.

WILLUM: Making tea.

AXEL: Ah. Tea. That's the word you were searching for.

TANSY: *(To* WILLUM.*)* Yes, I'm making the tea, don't worry.

WILLUM: *(Glancing about.)* Good. Good.

TANSY: Are you all right?

WILLUM: I'm all right. It's just that I'm a little—. I'm a little—.

AXEL: Teapot?

TANSY: Will you shut up?

WILLUM: Nervous. I'm a little nervous.

AXEL: Don't be silly. *(Checks watch.)* Zero hour, Kemp, we gotta get going, here. *(He goes to the window.)*

KEMP'S VOICE: Right, then—places, everyone. Break a leg. And, God, I wish I could be there with you kids tonight.

AXEL: *(Looking out window.)* He's coming. *(Starting the tape and replacing the books.)* He's coming, Kemp. See you later.

KEMP'S VOICE: Right. "March on, join bravely, let us to't pell-mell—."

AXEL: *(Going to the answering-machine.)* Kemp.

KEMP'S VOICE: "If not to heaven, then hand in hand—." *(But* AXEL *has banished him with the push of a button.)*

AXEL: All right. We ready? *(Everyone affects a nonchalant pose.)*

WILLUM: What if we forget something?

AXEL: *(Not having considered this.)* Oh? I don't know. Then we—*wing* it.

WILLUM: Oh, great. (RICK *enters, in fine spirits, attache case in hand.)*

RICK: Hi.

WILLUM: Hi, Rick.

TANSEY & AXEL: Hi, Rick.

RICK: Hi. *(To* WILLUM.*)* Hey, I got us some cards printed. *(He opens the attache case and dumps several pounds of calling-cards on the end-table.)*

AXEL: *(Taking a card and reading it.)* "Rick Steadman and Willum Cubbert: Architects and Best Friends." Very nice. How many've you got, there?

RICK: Twenty thousand.

AXEL: Uh-huh.

RICK: Ought to hold us awhile.

AXEL: Until the next Ice Age, anyway.

RICK: *(To* WILLUM, *who is reading one of the cards in dismay.)* What do you say, bud? Hey? Clam got your tongue?

WILLUM: Wha—?

RICK: Hey, where's this special dinner and all? We still doeen' that?

WILLUM: What?

TANSY: Sure. Nothing fancy—just a good old Terre Haute dinner. The kind we grew up on.

AXEL: That's right.

RICK: Good. 'Cause I invited somebody. Is anybody in the bathroom?

WILLUM: Rick—wait.

RICK: What?

WILLUM: You invited somebody? For when?

RICK: She didn't say. We should prob'ly just start. I'll be right back. *(He exits.)*

WILLUM: Give me strength.

TANSY: Who would he invite?

AXEL: Who knows? The printer's daughter.

WILLUM: What should we do?

AXEL: We have no choice. *(To* TANSY.*)* You're leaving in the morning, right?

TANSY: Right.

AXEL: So we go ahead. We just can't waste any time. If some local shows up here, we've had it.

WILLUM: *"Clam* got your tongue."

AXEL: What?

WILLUM: Rick just said, *"Clam* got your tongue?" I don't know if I can make it.

TANSY: You will, kid.

WILLUM: Yeah?

TANSY: Sure. You got the stuff.

WILLUM: *(Still worried.)* All right. (RICK *reenters, shirttail protruding from his fly.)*

RICK: *(Singing to himself.)* ". . . Venus . . . in blue jeans . . . Mona Lisa with a pony tail . . ."

WILLUM: Rick, who did you invite? (RICK *raises and lowers his eyebrows, as if to say, "A surprise." A teapot in the kitchen begins to whistle on the boil.)*

TANSY: I'll get it.

RICK: What's that?

AXEL: Mother's whistler.

WILLUM: Thought we'd have some tea.

RICK: We eateen' pretty soon? I'm starved.

AXEL: Pretty soon.

WILLUM: These traditional meals, you don't want to rush 'em.

AXEL: What were you singing there, minute ago?

RICK: "Venus in Blue Jeans."

AXEL: Ah.

RICK: You wanna hear it? I'm learneen' it on the tambourine. *(Before anyone can stop him, he picks up his tambourine and, focusing intently on some open music, he hums a lengthy introduction, then sings.)* "She's Venus . . . in Blue Jeans . . . Mona Lisa with a pony tail . . . She's a walkeen', talkeen'—*(He hits the tambourine once.)* work of art . . . She's the girl who stole my heart—." *(He puts the tambourine away again.)* That's all I know so far.

AXEL: That's interesting.

RICK: That's my favorite song. Next to "Nancy."

AXEL: What's "Nancy"? How does that go?

RICK: It's a comic strip.

AXEL: Oh . . . oh, yes. (TANSY *enters with the tea-tray—pot, cups, saucers and additives.)*

TANSY: Here we are. Tea-time.

WILLUM: Ah!

AXEL: Well, aren't we civilized.

TANSY: Why, of course. *(Offering* RICK *a cup.)* Rick?

RICK: Thanks. Are we goeen' to eat, sometime?

TANSY: Won't be long now.

RICK: Good.

TANSY: Cream?

RICK: Nah.

TANSY: Lemon?

RICK: 'Kay. *(He takes a lemon slice.)*

AXEL: We were just talking about our favorite old songs, and things.

TANSY: Oh, my. *(To* RICK.) You use sugar?

RICK: Sure. *(He takes a spoonful.)*

AXEL: Memories, memories.

TANSY: *(To* RICK.) Sand?

RICK: *(As if unsure he has heard.)* Hunh?

TANSY: Sand? *(Pointing to each of two bowls.)* Sugar on the left, sand on the right.

RICK: *(Pause.)* No, I'm fine. Thanks. *(He watches the tray as it passes to the others.)*

TANSY: Axel?

AXEL: *(Taking a cup.)* 'nk you.

TANSY: *(To* WILLUM) And—?

WILLUM: *(Taking a cup.)* Yes. Thanks.

TANSY: Oh, yes. Those old songs—take you right back. Just the other day, I—I'm sorry, Ax. Here.

AXEL: *(Helping himself.)* Just get some cream, here. And a little sugar —a-and some sand. *(He stirs all three into his tea.)*

WILLUM: *(To* TANSY.) What were you saying?

TANSY: Oh, just that I was listening to the radio the other day—*(To* WILLUM.) anything?

WILLUM: Just sand, thanks. *(He takes several spoonfuls of sand, stirs happily.)*

TANSY: —and what should come on but some old thing I haven't heard since high school. *(Adds lemon and sand to her own tea.)*

AXEL: Your tea is superb, incidentally.

WILLUM: *(Sipping.)* Mm!

TANSY: Is it?

WILLUM: Yes, indeed.

TANSY: *(Sips.)* Mm. Not so bad.

WILLUM: So what was on the radio?

TANSY: Oh, some old rock-'n'-roll song by Rip Delahoussaye and His All Girl Band. Remember them?

AXEL: Rip Delahoussaye. Sure.

WILLUM: Hey, they don't write songs like those any more. "Bumout"?

AXEL: "Bumout", yep. And "Dive Boppin' Mama"?

TANSY: "I Lost My Baby to the Great Big Train"?

WILLUM: Sure.

AXEL: Great songs.

WILLUM: Good times.

TANSY: And remember some of those old t.v. shows? "Herd Busters"?

AXEL: "Herd Busters". We used to listen to that on the *ra*dio. *(Deep, thrilling radio voice.)* "Out of the West they came—six tall men on a single horse!"

WILLUM: That's right. And remember "Furball and Snorkey"?

TANSY: Sure. With his friend Bunghead the Clown.

AXEL: And Sphinctre the Dog! That's right.

WILLUM: Yeah.

AXEL: That's right.

WILLUM: Boy. Childhood in Terre Haute.

TANSY: *(Nostalgically.)* No kidding. Do you—? I can remember—every year, right after the first snowfall, my father would take his old scatter-gun down from the mantel, go out into the woods, and see if he couldn't bring down a plane.

AXEL: Yeah. . . .

WILLUM: *(With a chuckle.)* Man, some of the things. *(To* RICK.) You ever go to pork-dances? They'd make us all go, us kids. We'd have to slow-dance all night with these big slabs of meat. It was supposed to be—preparation for later life, or something.

AXEL: Who knows.

WILLUM: I don't know.

AXEL: And did you ever—? Every Christmas, our family, we'd take this, really, it was the intestine of a sheep—and we'd stuff it full of this spicy sausage-meat.

WILLUM: Oh, yeah?

AXEL: *(Warmly.)* Yeah. *(Pause.)* That old sheep'd get so mad.

WILLUM: Well, sure she would.

AXEL: Got to where she'd know when Christmas was coming every year. We'd find her hiding.

WILLUM: Sure.

TANSY: Or we'd go out and dig in the snow, and see if we couldn't find ourselves some bananas.

RICK: What?

TANSY: *(As she exits to the kitchen.)* Oh, we had this crazy notion we wanted to start an orchestra. *(She exits.)*

WILLUM: La, la.

AXEL: Remember Old Man Wormsley?

WILLUM: *(Warmly.)* Nope.

AXEL: *(Happily.)* Me neither. (TANSY *enters with a steaming drum of hot tar.)*

TANSY: Rick? Boiling hot tar all over your face?

RICK: Not right now, thanks. (TANSY *exits.)*

WILLUM: So, Rick—

WILLUM & AXEL: *(Loud falsetto.)* Yeep! Yeep! Yeep!

WILLUM: —how would you compare Terre Haute life with what you're used to?

RICK: 'Bout the same.

WILLUM: Oh. . . . (TANSY *enters with saucers and two kinds of food-stuff, all on a tray.*)

TANSY: Here we go. *(To* RICK.) Saucer? *(He takes one.)* And—just help yourself.

RICK: What are those?

TANSY: Just our traditional appetizer—garbanzos and rusks.

RICK: Oh. *(He takes a rusk, then spoons a garbanzo or two onto it. He lifts it, but the garbanzos roll off onto his saucer. He tries again, balancing them precariously.)* They kinda roll around on there, don't they? *(They drop off again.)* Here. Wait a minute. *(He takes a second rusk; then, with a rusk in each hand, he pounces on the errant garbanzos, trapping them between improvised rusk-jaws.)* There we go. *(He takes a bite.)* Not bad. *(Wisely.)* That's really true, though. Food really tastes better when you catch it yourself, y'know? That's what my father always said. Departed father, I should say.

TANSY: *(Suddenly ashamed.)* Oh, Rick. When did he die?

RICK: *(Doesn't she have ears?)* He didn't die. He just departed.

TANSY: Oh. . . .

RICK: Yeah, I woke up one morneen', and he was gone. I still remember, 'cause it was the day after I got my tambourine.

TANSY: Uh-huh . . .

AXEL: Yeah. . . .

WILLUM: *(Crossing to* AXEL *for more tea. Between his teeth.)* What now, Ax?

AXEL: *(Smiling, pouring.)* Oh, something a little stronger, I think.

WILLUM: All right.

RICK: This is great.

WILLUM: Yeah.

RICK: Good old Terre Haute.

WILLUM: Right.

RICK: I can hardly wait till it gets winter, so we can shoot some planes and stuff some sheep!

WILLUM: Ax—.

AXEL: Right. Oh—Old Man Winter. Whew! *(To* RICK.) I hope you brought your gear.

RICK: Huh?

AXEL: You know—parkas, space heaters. Mukluks.

RICK: What?

AXEL: Well, we'll get you some, don't worry.

WILLUM: *(Catching on.)* Oh! Oh, sure.

AXEL: 'Cause it's gonna get pret-ty mean out there, starting—*(Checks watch.)* well, about now, really.

WILLUM: Oh, it's not that bad. A few months of howling, bleak nothingness. But—there's no reason you shouldn't—survive. *We* did.

TANSY: Sure. *We've* been lucky. *(Her expression changes.)* Well, luckier than—the others.

RICK: What? Others?

TANSY: Oh, Rick.

AXEL: This house used to be *filled* with people.

TANSY: Yes . . .

AXEL: Gone, now.

WILLUM: They couldn't take the winter.

RICK: Who couldn't?

WILLUM: *You* know. The old.

AXEL: The young.

TANSY: The sick.

AXEL: *(To* TANSY.) Who do you miss the most?

TANSY: The sick, I guess.

AXEL: Yeah.

WILLUM: *(To* RICK.) Oh, Rick. You should have been here.

TANSY: This house used to ring with the laughter of the sick.

WILLUM: No more.

TANSY: No. . . .

WILLUM: No more.

RICK: What happened?

WILLUM: Oh—starvation.

TANSY: Marauding savages from Indianapolis.

WILLUM: Yes. . . . And forest beasts, on the prowl—desperate for food for their hibernating young.

RICK: Are you kiddeen'? Some *beasts?*

WILLUM: Oh, yes.

RICK: What did you do when there was *beasts* comeen' around?

AXEL: Well, if all else failed, one of the sick would go out there, and offer himself up.

RICK: Huh.

AXEL: How are you feeling?

RICK: Fine.

AXEL: Yeah?

RICK: What kind of beasts are they?

WILLUM: Oh . . . what. Coyotes.

AXEL: Wolverines.

TANSY: Mastodons. (AXEL *and* WILLUM *look at her.)* Sometimes.

RICK: Oh, yeah. We got those.

WILLUM: You do? *Mas*todons?

RICK: Yeah, I think. Don't they have, like, real hairy palms, or sometheen'?

WILLUM: I'm not sure.

RICK: Any pigs?

WILLUM: What? Pigs?

RICK: Yeah.

WILLUM: No. Listen, we're talking about—.

RICK: Good. 'Cause those are the ones I hate. Whenever I see a pig, like, in a movie or sometheen'? Forget it. I'm outta there. I can't take those suckers.

AXEL: Well, we do get *some* pigs.

WILLUM: Quite a few, really.

TANSY: Big, giant—.

AXEL: *Mut*ant pigs.

WILLUM: They'd as soon kill you as look at you.

RICK: Really?

TANSY: Big, hairy things. *(The kitchen timer sounds again.)* Woop! Dinner time! *(She exits.)*

WILLUM: Oh, boy.

AXEL: *(To* RICK.) Man, am I ready for some chow. How about you?

RICK: Oh, yeah. I'm starveen'.

AXEL: Great.

RICK: Pigs, huh? (WILLUM *and* AXEL *nod.* TANSY *enters with a huge tureen; puts it on the table.)* What are we haveen'?

TANSY: Wait, Rick.

AXEL: Wait.

TANSY: First—a little surprise.

RICK: Huh?

TANSY: *(Uncovering a tureen.) Ta-da!*

WILLUM: Oh, boy.

AXEL: An apple core!

WILLUM: Oh, we're gonna have some fun now! (TANSY *carefully sets the core upright on the table.)*

AXEL: *(To* RICK.) You ever do this?

RICK: What are we doeen'?

WILLUM: *(As they excitedly gather around the core.)* Gonna watch this baby turn *brown.*

AXEL: Yeah!

RICK: Why?

TANSY: Oh—it's just our way.

RICK: Oh. *(Pause.)* Then we're not goeen' to eat till it turns brown?

TANSY: Right.

RICK: Because it's your *way?*

WILLUM & AXEL: Right.

RICK: Oh. . . .

WILLUM: Okay, okay. Shh! *(They all stare at the apple core. Fifteen or twenty seconds pass. Occasionally someone takes a sip of tea.)*

RICK: I think maybe my side's turneen' brown a little bit. *(More seconds pass.)* No, maybe not. *(More seconds.)* Your side turneen' brown? *(One or two of the others shake their heads.)* Little bit? No? *(Pause.)* 'Kay. *(He watches a bit longer.)* C'mon, apple cord. *(Pause.)* Yeah, you wouldn't of thought this would be that much fun, but it really kind of is, isn't it? *(The others keep staring, hoping they have heard incorrectly.)* Better than watcheen' chalk, that's for sure. You could watch chalk forever and it would never do anything neat like turn brown. This is great.

WILLUM: *(Seeing that this isn't working.)* Uh—Tansy—? Maybe you should check—.

TANSY: *(Taking her cue.)* Ah! Sounds like the old kitchen timer! Time for dinner! *(She goes to the kitchen.)*

RICK: What?

AXEL: Oh—too bad.

RICK: We don't get to finish watcheen' the apple cord?

WILLUM: No. *(He throws the apple core away.)*

RICK: Aw. Maybe we could do another one later.

AXEL: Sure.

RICK: Oh, boy! This is the most fun night I had since I got here!

WILLUM: Axel—.

AXEL: Tansy!

TANSY: *(Off.)* Coming!

RICK: Oh, you know what else would be fun right now? While we're waiteen'? How would you guys like to see some—*mime!*

AXEL & WILLUM: *Tansy!*

TANSY: *(Offstage.)* Here it comes!

AXEL: Mm, boy! I smell my favorite! (TANSY *enters with another covered dish.)*

RICK: What're we haveen'?

TANSY: *(Triumphantly lifting the lid.)* Warm water and cottage cheese!

AXEL & WILLUM: Mmmmmm!

RICK: *(Looking at it.)* Warm water and cottage cheese?

WILLUM: You bet.

AXEL: You'll be seeing this two, three times a day, till spring.

RICK: *(He stares at the repast.* AXEL *and* WILLUM *exchange hopeful glances.)* Warm water and cottage *cheese?*

WILLUM: Anything wrong?

RICK: Not really, but—.

WILLUM: Hmm?

RICK: But that's just so funny, though. This keeps happeneen'.

WILLUM: What?

RICK: This is the same thing I had for lunch.

WILLUM: *(Pause.)* What?

RICK: Yeah. It was good, though. I could really go for some more, by this time. *(He takes some cottage cheese.)*

WILLUM: *(Through his teeth.)* Ax̲el.

AXEL: Don't worry. Wait. *Wait.* I hear something.

WILLUM: Huh?

AXEL: *(Getting up, alarmed.)* Hit the lights. *Hurry.* (WILLUM *does.* AXEL, *at the window.)* Dammit, I was afraid of this. It's them. They're here.

WILLUM: Who?

AXEL: The *pigs.*

RICK: The pigs?

TANSY: *(Catching on.)* Oh. Oh no. So soon.

AXEL: Looks like a couple hundred. Christ, the place is crawling with 'em.

RICK: *(Running to the window.)* What are they doeen'?

AXEL: Woop! They're gone.

RICK: *(Looking out the window.) Fast* little dudes.

AXEL: You know it.

TANSY: Thank God they've gone. (WILLUM *turns the lights back on.)*

AXEL: They'll be back. And next time they won't be alone.

RICK: What were they doeen'?

AXEL: *(Sounding more and more like a cop.)* Squealing. Grunting. The usual. Looked like some of 'em had broken into a house already.

WILLUM: Yeah?

AXEL: *(Nods.)* Their mouths were all covered with blood and cottage cheese.

WILLUM: Horrible.

TANSY: I'm worried.

AXEL: Sure you're worried. *(Lighting a cigarette.)* You're worried big, and I don't blame you. Rick, it's time we let you in on something. This is bad. *Real* bad. You see, Willum was once badly bitten by *(Gesturing out the window.)* one of those palookas. He doesn't talk about it much. You don't talk much when you've been pig-bit. But if we don't level with you now, you're gonna find out the hard way. You see, sometimes—. You want to tell him, Willum?

WILLUM: *(Looking vaguely despairing while trying to catch up.)* Not really. *(A signal from* ALEX.*)* No, you go ahead.

AXEL: Well, you see, sometimes now, when the moon is full, Willum—. *(Making himself say it.)* Sometimes he turns into a—*(Turns away as if to say, "You know the rest.")* well. *(Pause.)*

RICK: That's horrible!

AXEL: I know.

RICK: He turns into a *well?*

AXEL: What? No.

RICK: Huh?

AXEL: No. Into a pig.

RICK: *Oh.* I was gonna *say.*

AXEL: You've never seen anything like it.

RICK: 'Cause I never heard of *any*body turneen' into a *well.*

AXEL: Well, no—.

RICK: But a pig, no, that's different, that's kind of like—. *(*TANSY *has turned away, trying to keep from laughing.)* What's wrong with that girl?

AXEL: *(Going to her.)* She's just—.

TANSY: *(Acting, still turned away.)* It's just so horrible!

AXEL: Poor kid. We've all had to live with this damn thing. *(Going to* WILLUM, *who has sat on the couch trying to look despondent.)* Willum. Was it wrong of me to tell him?

WILLUM: No. . . . No. I'm glad you told him. It's time he knew. Oh, the shame of it . . . the *shame.* *(He runs a shaking hand through his hair.)* Christ, I could kill for some slop!

AXEL: *(Grabbing his shoulders.)* Be *strong. Fight* it, Willum!

WILLUM: Yes. . . . *(Staggering about.)* Yes, I've got to be *(He snorts loudly twice.)* strong.

TANSY: *(Joining in.)* Willum!

WILLUM: As long as I have friends like *(Snorts twice.)* like you, I can *(Snort!)*—I can *(Snort!)* I *(Snorts several times.)* Oh! Oh, no! *(He drops to his knees, lunging for Rick.* TANSY *screams.)*

AXEL: *(Grabbing* WILLUM.) Help me, Tansy! Hold him! *(She does.* WILLUM *snorts, struggling.)* Rick! Take off! Get out of here, quick!

RICK: Huh?

AXEL: *Run,* I tell you! Run as if your life depended on it. Then, by all that's holy, get in your car and drive! Drive away from this godforsaken hell. Drive and drive, and try to forget the nameless horror that you've witnessed here tonight! *(RICK just stands there.) Now,* Rick! *(WILLUM squeals.)* What are you waiting for? Run!

RICK: Are you *kid*deen'?

AXEL: Don't be a hero, Rick! Go! Go, while you still have the chance!

RICK: And miss him turneen' into a *pig?* No *way!*

AXEL: All right. Uh—all *right—.*

WILLUM & TANSY: *A*xel—.

AXEL: Just *wait* a minute! All right! *(Improvising wildly.)* You want to stay, *stay.* But believe me, it's not gonna be pretty. There's only one way to stop this thing from happening now, *(Confronting* WILLUM.) and you know what I'm talking about!

WILLUM: *Huh?*

AXEL: Oh, sure. Oh, *sure, I* know—you'd like to spare your friend here this grisly spectacle, but *Will*um—there's *just no choice!*

WILLUM & TANSY: Huh?

AXEL: *(To Rick.)* Brace yourself, Rick. You're about to see us as we really are. Ugly. Primitive. And when this is over you'll never look at any of us the same way again. But it's the only way we can fight this thing—with hideous pagan ritual! *(During the following, AXEL hurries about the room gathering props—a trash can to use as a drum, an animal skin, and so on.)*

RICK: *(To WILLUM.)* "Hideous pagan ritual"?

WILLUM: Well—uh, fairly hideous, yeah.

AXEL: *(Handing RICK and WILLUM two napkin-rings each.)* Here, put these on. Tansy, see what—check out the closet.

TANSY: *(Going to the closet.)* Whatever you say.

RICK: *(Frowning at his napkin-rings.)* Put these—?

AXEL: Around—over your ears.

WILLUM: *(Grateful for the tip.)* Right.

RICK: *(As he and WILLUM put on the rings.)* This—is this your way?

WILLUM: Yeah.

RICK: That's what I thought.

TANSY: *(Coming from the closet with two dust mops.)* How are these?

AXEL: Great. Do we have a live goat?

TANSY: No.

AXEL: Well. We'll do without. Ready? *(To* RICK.) Now, *don't be fright-
ened!* (He turns a tin trash can into a conga drum, loudly beating out
what he considers a wild tattoo.)
"Hey! Walla! Walla! Walla!
Hey! Walla! Walla! Walla!"
(TANSY *and* WILLUM *begin leaping about selfconsciously,* TANSY *using
the dust mops as pompoms; they grimace and shout, doing their best to
look "hideous.")*

TANSY & WILLUM: *"Hey!* Walla! Walla! Walla!
Hey! Walla! Walla! Walla!"

AXEL: "Soo-*ee!* Soo-*ee!"*

TANSY & WILLUM: "Soo-*ee!* Soo-*ee!"*

AXEL: "Pig-god! Pig-god! Go away!
Come again some other day!
Pig-god, pig—"
C'*mon!*
"Pig-god—"

TANSY, WILLUM & AXEL: "—pig-god, go away!"

AXEL: Rick!

TANSY, WILLUM & AXEL: "Come again—"

ALL FOUR: "—some other day!"

AXEL: *"Hey!* Walla! Walla! Walla!
Hey! Walla! Walla! Walla!"

ALL FOUR: *"Hey!* Walla! Walla! Walla!
Hey! Walla! Walla! Walla!"

AXEL: *(Demonstrating.) "Wave* your *arms* from *side* to *side!"*

ALL FOUR: *(Waving their arms.) "Wave* your *arms* from *side* to *side!"*

AXEL: *"Show* those *gods* we've *got* some *pride!"*

ALL FOUR: *"Show* those *gods* we've *got* some *pride!"* (AXEL *points to* WILLUM.)

WILLUM: Uh—*"walk around* the *ta*ble, *twice!"*

ALL FOUR: *(Following* WILLUM *around the table.)* "Walk around the *ta*ble, *twice!"*

TANSY: *"Take* some *sugar? Take* some *spice!"*

ALL FOUR: *(Tossing sugar and salt in the air.)* *"Take* some *sugar? Take* some *spice!"*

WILLUM: "Oh, *grab* a *cup* of *cottage cheese!"*

ALL FOUR: *(Doing so.)* *"Grab* a *cup* of *cottage cheese!"*

AXEL: *(Running to the open window.)* *"Throw* it *out* on *Mister Trees!"*

ALL FOUR: *(Hurling their cottage cheese out the window.)* "Throw it *out* on *Mister Trees!"*

TANSY: *(Marching back to the center of the room.) Now* we *march* back *to* our *place—!"*

ALL FOUR: *(Marching back.)* "Now we *march* back *to* our *place—!"*

RICK: *(Leaping to the middle of the room and pounding himself playfully on the head.)* "Jump *around* and *hit* your *head!"*

THE OTHERS: *"Jump a*—"

RICK: C'mon! "Jump a—"

ALL FOUR: *(Jumping and hitting.)* *"—round* and *hit* your *head!"*

RICK: *(Leaping from the room.)* "Let's all *jump* around *in* the *ki*tchen!"

WILLUM: What're we—? (AXEL *gestures helplessly as everyone follows* RICK *to the kitchen.)*

ALL FOUR: *"Let's all jump around in the kitchen!"*

RICK: *(Offstage. With a clanking accompaniment.)* *"Hit some pots and pans, let's go!"*

ALL FOUR: *(Shouting above a deafening clatter.)* *"Hit some pots and pans, let's go!"*

WILLUM: *(Offstage.)* Rick—.

RICK: *(Leaping back into the room.)* *"Go real fast on just one leg!"*

ALL FOUR: *(Back in, hopping.)* *"Go real fast on just one leg!"*

WILLUM: *(Grabbing the ball.)* *"As we end our lit-tle rhyme—!"*

TANSY, WILLUM, AXEL: *"As we end our lit-tle rhyme—!"*

WILLUM: *(Hopping around in a little circle.)* *"Do a circle one last time!"*

RICK: Hi, Tocky.

TANSY, WILLUM, AXEL: *(Hopping in a circle.)* *"Do a circle—"*

AXEL: *"—one last—"* (TANSY, WILLUM *and* AXEL *stop, now facing front, realizing what they have seen in the doorway on their last swing around. It is indeed* WALDGRAVE, *looking surprisingly intimidating for someone who is covered with cottage cheese.)*

WALDGRAVE: *(With quiet fury.)* I presume someone here can explain why I have cottage cheese all over me.

RICK: *(Making a stab at it.)* Um, is it your way?

WALDGRAVE: You—don't you start again with me!

RICK: What's wrong, Tocky?

WALDGRAVE: What!

RICK: What's wrong, Tocky?

WALDGRAVE: All right, you say it right, goddammit! I've had a very bad day, and I'm going to hear you say it right just once. Say it!

RICK: What do you mean?

WALDGRAVE: "What's wrong, *Ticky!*"

RICK: Hunh?

WALDGRAVE: "What's wrong, *Ticky!*"

RICK: Notheen's wrong. *(Shrugs.)* Why are you calleen' me Ticky?

WALDGRAVE: Goddammit. God*dam*mit!

RICK: No, that's okay. Call me Ticky if it makes you feel good.

WALDGRAVE: It doesn't make me feel good!

RICK: Then I wouldn't.

WALDGRAVE: *(Hand in coat.)* Where are my pills?

RICK: No, maybe not, 'cause people might mix us up if you call me Ticky, 'cause that sounds kind of like your nickname of Tocky, y'know? You're right. Okay, so then you just call me whatever you want to, okay?

WALDGRAVE: Jesus.

WILLUM: Here—look—.

RICK: "Jesus"? That would make me sound like I was from the Bible.

WILLUM: Rick—.

RICK: Or—or on a baseball team, at least.

WILLUM: Rick—.

RICK: I don't know—"Jesus Steadman." That's—.

WILLUM: Rick, *please.*

RICK: No, but no, okay. So you want to call me Jesus, then, and I'll just keep calleen' you—uh, Tacky?

WALDGRAVE: Tocky!

TANSY: *(Gently correcting him.)* Ticky.

WALDGRAVE: Ticky. Goddammit.

WILLUM: *(Trying to calm things down.)* Mr. Waldgrave, let's just—first of all just tell me why you're here.

WALDGRAVE: Why am I—! I was supposed to come here for dinner!

WILLUM: For *din*ner?

WALDGRAVE: What are you—? Isn't this from you? *(He pulls a note from his pocket.)* My secretary gave me this—"Dinner Cubbert's tonight."

WILLUM: This—there's some mixup.

WALDGRAVE: I tried to call back, but all I could get was your damn ma*chine.* And instead of a message, you know what you got on there? Somebody singing a song about, "There's something in my pocket that belongs upon my face!" You listen all the way through and it turns out to be "a great big Brownie smile!" I mean, what the *hell!*

WILLUM: I don't know who called you, Mr. Waldgrave, but it wasn't me.

WALDGRAVE: Then who the hell *was* it?

RICK: Surprise!

WILLUM: *You?*

RICK: Me!

WILLUM: Oh, Rick.

WALDGRAVE: Oh, Jesus.

RICK: Whichever. *(To* WILLUM.) Yeah, you said it was a special dinner, so I called Tocky's secretary.

WALDGRAVE: *(To* WILLUM.) Dammit, I thought maybe you wanted to talk about the Regency, for once. You remember the Regency? The Regency Ho*tel?*

RICK: *(To* WALDGRAVE.) Oh, *right!* What did you think of that *chim*ney, hey?

WALDGRAVE: What chimney?

RICK: The one on the left.

WALDGRAVE: What?

RICK: Did he blow a cigarette through it for *you?*

WALDGRAVE: What?

RICK: Did he blow a cigarette through it for *you?*

WALDGRAVE: Did he blow a cigarette through *what* for me?

RICK: The chimney.

WALDGRAVE: What chimney?

RICK: The one on the left.

WALDGRAVE: Cubbert!

WILLUM: Rick.

WALDGRAVE: *(Bearing in on* WILLUM.) All right, look. *I* don't know what's going on here. I'm invited to dinner, I step out of my car and get pelted with cottage cheese; then I come up here, I find my architect jumping around, things on his head, acting like some cheerleader from Mars, or something. Well and good. I don't know from that; I don't want to know. What I know is, I now have a son who's afraid of closets; my wife, if my wife even *sees* a paper bag, she gets so nervous she has to break every dish in the house; and I have a hotel which is now one week behind *sche*dule! I mean, *Je*sus—what am I supposed to *do?*

RICK: How should *I* know? (WALDGRAVE *glares at* RICK, *then returns to* WILLUM.)

WALDGRAVE: Well, I tell you, pal—I've had it! This is it for me. *(Taking a folded paper from his coat.)* You see this? This is our contract. *(He rips it in half.) That's* for your disappearing act—*(He rips it again.) that's* for your army buddy—*(And again.)* that's for your lousy designs—*(And again.)* and that's for your cottage cheese! I'm not telling anybody about this, because anyway nobody would believe me, but I am for damn sure getting myself another architect! *(He starts out.)*

RICK: Oh, hey, wait! You want another architect? *(He grabs one of the newly-printed cards.)* Here's my card. Oh, wait a minute—. *(He quickly tears off the bottom half.)* 'Kay, here. (WALDGRAVE, *not taking the card, gives him one last withering look, and is gone.* RICK *hurries to the window.)* What was the matter? I tore off the Cubbert part. *(He watches after* WALDGRAVE.)

WILLUM: *(This having pushed him smoothly over the brink.) Out* you go. That was it. Goodbye. *(He is quickly and efficiently packing* RICK*'s things.)* Maybe this is wrong of me, but at this point I'm ready to take the consequences—a lifetime of guilt, an eternity in hell, either one sounds just fine. I don't owe you my life. Okay? That was my mistake; I let things go this far because I thought I owed you my life. But I don't. Nobody owes anybody his life. Period. So here, I'm packing for you—*(As he packs each item.)* packing your tambourine —and your brother Bob's credit cards—and this pic—*(Looking at it.)* what is this—? your autographed picture of Hugh Downs—everything. I wish things had been different. I wish to hell we had really hit it off, and married each other's sister, and all that other M-G-M stuff, but that's just not the way it is. And so—goodbye. *(He has finished* *packing.)* This hasn't been easy to say, but at least—now you know how I feel.

RICK: *(Turning back from the window, seemingly startled to find* WIL-LUM *looking at him.)* I'm sorry, what? Were you talkeen' to me?

WILLUM: Rick—don't tell me you weren't listening.

RICK: I was lookeen' out there at—I thought it was a pig, but I guess it was just a rock.

WILLUM: You're leaving now, Rick. *(Puts the suitcase down.)* Here. Go.

RICK: Well—what do you mean?

WILLUM: I mean go. Go away. Go out. Don't come back.

RICK: You mean—what?

WILLUM: Pick up your suitcase. Leave. Don't come back.

RICK: Uh—well, you mean—?

WILLUM: Before I count to three. One—*(Suddenly* RICK *is in the door-way, suitcase in hand.)*

RICK: *(Wisely, head to one side.)* Hey. I can take a hint. *(And with a snort he is gone.* WILLUM *drops into a chair.)*

TANSY: Willum—you don't know how long I've waited to see you do something like that.

AXEL: Yeah, kid, that was great. And listen, with that hotel business, I don't know how you feel about that, but if you ask me—. (WILLUM *has put his face in his hands. He begins to shake.)*

TANSY: *(Worried.)* Willum—? *(But* WILLUM, *for almost the first time since we've known him, is laughing. A falsetto giggle is erupting from him, muffled at first, then louder and louder. He turns his face up-ward, clutching his sides and laughing the unstoppable, cosmic laugh-ter of one who, by some chance astral projection, has suddenly found himself watching the pathetic, hilarious lunacy of his own existence from a plateau usually reserved only for the gods. And for us, of course.)* Willum, are you laughing?

WILLUM: *(Through tears of laughter.)* "I presume—" *(Laughs.)* "I presume* someone here can tell me why—*(Laughs.)*—why I'm covered with cottage cheese!" *(All three laugh now.)* And here, we're all hopping around with—with rings on our—. *(He gestures toward his ears, laughing. They laugh.)* Oh. Oh, mercy.

TANSY: You're all right, then?

WILLUM: Yeah, I'm—I mean, I think my hair's gonna start coming in white, now, but—*(Rather surprised.) yeah.* You know? It's pe*cu*liar.

TANSY: What?

WILLUM: I think I must—I think maybe I'm glad I lost that job. Is that—?

TANSY: Willum, that was the worst job you ever had.

WILLUM: Was it? It was, wasn't it?

TANSY: Yep.

WILLUM: Why didn't you say anything?

TANSY: I couldn't do that. You had to see it yourself.

WILLUM: I wonder if I ever would have, if all this—this ridiculous *lun*acy hadn't happened.

TANSY: Maybe not.

WILLUM: That's *true.* You know? If I had never—if Rick hadn't been here. Yeah. Whaddaya know. *(Laughs.)* Rick Steadman. I should thank Rick Steadman.

AXEL: *(Starting toward the door.)* Maybe I can still catch him.

WILLUM: *Don't*—you—*move! (They all laugh.)* You know what? Let's go to dinner, I'll take you to dinner.

AXEL: I've got to see a show.

WILLUM: Oh, right. *(To* TANSY.*)* Tansy?

TANSY: *(Extending her palms to say, "I'm ready for anything.")* Hey!

WILLUM: Great. *(Getting* TANSY's *coat and his own.)* I'm gonna take you to dinner, and then I'm gonna come back here, I'm gonna put all my Regency stuff through the *shredder,* and then—*(Stopping.)* then what? I don't *know.* I guess it's back to housing develop—*(As his eyes light on the answering machine.)* Wait a minute. . . . *Wait* a *min*ute. . . . *(Pause. We can almost hear the pieces snapping into place.)*

AXEL: *(Trying not to smile.)* We're waiting.

WILLUM: You know what I could—? My God, it's suddenly so *ob*vious, the thing for me to do. *(To* AXEL.*)* You wanna hear? *(Throwing his portfolio together.)* Tomorrow morning when Red Graham calls, I say, "Yes, Red Graham, I will do your housing development in Alexandria, Virginia, thank you." Take off in the morning, set up shop out there, sooner or later I get myself another hotel, or I get something better than that—a mu*seum*—and this time it'll look, by God, the way *I* want it to. And between jobs—between jobs, on holidays, anytime I can get away—I'm gonna drive across that river to Washington, D.C.—and I'm gonna court Tansy till she cracks. *(Daring to look at her.)* What do you think of that?

TANSY: *(A little dazed.)* That . . . sounds like a reasonable plan. . . .

WILLUM: Great. I'll get the car. *(He goes.* TANSY *follows him to the door, then turns back to* AXEL, *pointing after* WILLUM *with the bouncy, rhythmic point one uses when trying to remember something.)*

TANSY: *(Finally.)* Marjorie Main.

AXEL: My thought exactly. *(A car honks outside, and* TANSY *is gone.* AXEL *goes to the window to wave them off. Then he hurries to the*

phone and starts pushing buttons, but before he can finish, it rings.)
Hello?

KEMP'S VOICE: Tell me some news.

AXEL: *Kemp?* I think we did it, babe.

KEMP'S VOICE: Yes?

AXEL: I think so. I think a hundred percent.

KEMP'S VOICE: *(Pleased.)* You don't say.

AXEL: Get up here, I'll tell you all about it—you downstairs?

KEMP'S VOICE: Yeah.

AXEL: Come on up. Maybe we can get schnockered before we see this turko.

KEMP'S VOICE: What're we seeing?

AXEL: Who remembers? *(He takes out his pad. The phone clicks off. Reading from his pad, sounding like the Voice of Doom.)* The Endless Plain. *(Composing his review.)* "The Endless Plain, in this reviewer's opinion, is plain endless." Not bad. *(He starts mixing drinks. There is a double knock at the door.)*

KEMP'S VOICE: All clear?

AXEL: It's open. *(The door opens. In the doorway, to our surprise, stands the gentleman we have come to know as* RICK STEADMAN. *Without glasses, freshly groomed, and in a tux, he looks—well, absolutely great.* AXEL *abandons his drinks to welcome him with an uncharacteristic embrace.)* Hey, there's the man! Oh, Kemp, you bastard, you were really pushing it! One more minute and I would've lost it, I swear!

KEMP: *(Stepping into the room, grinning.)* You know what is really hard? It's really hard to walk in here without—*(In* RICK'S *voice.)* "talkeen' like this all the time, y'know, hey?"

AXEL: I can imagine. I mean, for a week. My God. Poor Rick.

KEMP: Poor Rick, yes. I often wonder what he's really like, don't you?

AXEL: Hm?

KEMP: The real Rick Steadman. Up in Wisconsin.

AXEL: Nice fella, probably.

KEMP: Probably.

AXEL: He was nice for us, anyway. From all indications, tomorrow morning we should find Willum and his little weather woman heading toward the Washington sunset in double harness.

KEMP: That's good. Not a bad fellow, your friend Willum.

AXEL: He's all right. He just needed to have his life interfered with a little, that's all.

KEMP: Yes. Plus—.

AXEL: What?

KEMP: Well, this settles your score with Tansy, too, doesn't it?

AXEL: I don't know what you're talking about.

KEMP: Isn't this your "anonymous favor?"

AXEL: *(Offering him one.)* Cigar?

KEMP: You're not going to tell me?

AXEL: Going, going—.

KEMP: *(Taking it.)* All right.

AXEL: *(Finishing adjustments to his hair and tie.)* How do I look?

KEMP: Hideous.

AXEL: Good. Let's go.

KEMP: *(As* RICK.*)* "Okayy—hitteen' the old road, now." (AXEL *stops and looks back at the answering-machine, smiling at a thought.)*

AXEL: Hm.

KEMP: What?

AXEL: Oh, I was just wondering.

KEMP: What?

AXEL: What do you really think Willum will do, when he finds out there's no such person as Red Graham?

KEMP: *(As they leave, speaking in* RED*'s voice.)* "Well, son, *my* guess is, by that time he'll be so blamed happy he'll ferget t' be mad."

AXEL: That is my hope. *(The door closes behind them. An ancient fox-trot swells up. The lights fade.)*